HEALTH INSURANCE
SUCKS

To my wonderful & beautiful wife. Without her love and support this book would have never have come to pass. Thank you for everything you do for me, and for being my soulmate to the end of time.

HEALTH INSURANCE
SUCKS

JOHN BUTLER

AMERICA WILL BE
SILENCED
NO MORE

THE MORAL CASE FOR
BETTER BUSINESS HEALTHCARE

Printed in the United States of America
First printing, April 2021

First edition

ISBN: 978-0-578-85505-9

Cover Design: Jake Nordby
Interior Book Design: Ann Aubitz

Published by:

BENEFITS
CONSULTING

NOTE FROM THE AUTHOR

Do Not Pass by This Page

This book doesn't just offer solutions to the problems we face regarding health insurance and healthcare in this country. It offers a completely different framework of thinking regarding this subject. Here is the thought pattern approach offered within these pages.

- You must be open to any and all solutions without any biases toward one solution or another.
- You must be prepared to look at both the positives as well as the negatives within each solution described in this book.
- You must be willing to be laser-like precise within every analysis. Vagueness or sloppy analysis is not acceptable.
- You must set your mindset toward the standard of reducing health insurance costs, while increasing the healthcare benefits to employees.
- You must accept, as the ultimate "Standard of Value", a *set healthcare budget* that is fully under your control.

Since business healthcare has never been approached with this framework of thinking, I wanted to be clear about this thought process from the very beginning.
Thank you in advance!

John Butler

ADVANCED PRAISE

"John Butler's *Health Insurance Sucks* is a must-read for anyone who wants the truth about healthcare. John's passion for educating people in this arena is unparalleled, and his results are unmatched. John is more than a healthcare expert. He is the leader in this field – guiding, coaching, and mentoring people through the rough seas of an ever-changing and difficult-to-understand industry. John not only simplifies everything but he provides viable solutions that impact every individual and every business."
-Erik Therwanger – Founder & CEO of ThinkGREAT

"My company has worked with John Butler and his Team for a number of years on several different employee medical insurance programs. I can honestly state from my experience that no one is more dedicated than John personally to the conversion of America's Health Insurance Industry away from the monolithic, inflexible Fixed-Rate model. He has been a pioneer and researcher of optional approaches that cost less and that directly involve administrators and caregivers in giving participants guidance and hands-on assistance with finding treatment options from which they can choose when needed. He has definitely been "thinking outside of the box" to the benefit of the businesses and their employees that he serves."
-Michael Hansen - J&E Manufacturing CEO

TABLE OF CONTENTS

CHAPTER 1

HOW **NOT** TO DO IT

Everyone knows health insurance sucks. The biggest mistake most people make is bitching and complaining about it, rather than taking the time to find out how to make it *not* suck.

Over half of the people in the United States are currently insured through some kind of employer-sponsored health insurance. It's no secret that the premiums for both employers and their employees keep on rising while the insurance benefits are getting worse. **The deductibles and out-of-pocket medical costs are so high that employees around the country are going bankrupt, sometimes *even when they have insurance through their employer!***

I am not here to whine and moan along with the rest of the world. Nor am I here to sell you on a political program that will solve our problems in some far-off future. I am here with good news and a huge ray of hope for anyone who either owns a business or works for a business that provides healthcare.

The good news is that you can solve your health insurance woes *today*. After reading this book, you will:

1. Understand the innovative business-healthcare solutions that already exist around the country with proven track records of success.
2. Be able to connect with the proper solution partners for efficient implementation into your business.
3. Know the exact steps you need to take to save 20 to 40 percent or more in healthcare and health insurance costs within 120 days.

I'm going to be uncovering solutions that have already been formed and developed by innovative minds from all around the country. Healthcare for businesses has been such an incredibly complicated issue to deal with over the last few decades. But there are groundbreaking advancements by so many people in so many different fields, and the employers adopting these strategies are realizing better benefits for their employees while sometime saving as much as 50 percent to 60 percent on some occasions, depending on the employer's appetite for change.

How I Discovered the Solutions to Expensive Health Insurance

I realize these are bold claims, so let me tell you a little bit about who I am and how I discovered the strategies I'll be sharing with you in the pages ahead.

I have been in the financial and insurance industry since 1988. I started as a financial advisor and transitioned to the employee-benefits business in 1996. I started working with small to midsize employers analyzing which healthcare programs were best for my clients.

Operating as a broker in Minnesota for many years, I found myself choosing between four or five different insurance companies for my clients. If one insurance carrier increased a client's health insurance rates by 25 percent, I would shop the market and try to find better deals with the other insurance carriers. It became a spreadsheet comparison game as to which one would give the best deal to my employer clients.

I was never really given a satisfactory answer from any of the insurance companies as to why they needed to raise the rates so much each year. Many years, claims were well below what the total annual premiums had been, and yet clients would still receive a minimum of 6 to 8 percent increases (on average) every year. Employers had to repeatedly raise deductibles higher and higher to limit the premium increases. Over the years, I began to work with much larger size companies, and I came to realize that the same problems existed whether a company had 50, 500, or 5000 employees. In fact, I found out that most times, the problem actually got worse as the employee sizes got larger. Most people think that the problem gets smaller as a company grows in size. That's exactly what I believed to be true!

Yet, the country's average healthcare spend is now at $15,000 per employee per year (PEPY) and rising. We recently ran into a local company here in my home state of Minnesota that had 224 employees. Their average spend was $30,000 PEPY because their employee's claims were always difficult, and they were never given any reasonable solutions from their brokerage firm.

So, starting six years ago, I began digging deep to research why all of this was happening. I came to realize that the price increases were intentional by the insurance companies. They simply took the rules, put upon them by the government, and made sure that healthcare prices nationwide continued to rise. With no restrictions and or limitations on healthcare prices, they could simply increase their health insurance costs year after year, passing these higher premiums on to employers and their employees. Most of the products I was providing to small and midsize companies in my former broker role paid the insurance companies the highest profit margins of any product that they offered in the marketplace. And the brokers and brokerage firms were being financially incentivized to keep employers within this broken system.

I sadly came to the realization that I was simply part of the problem. Embarrassing to say the least!

My six years of research took me to places that I never even imagined. I truly can't take any of the credit for the incredible innovations that have taken place over the last five to ten years. What I did discover, though, was that there are business-healthcare systems (already in place) delivering consistent savings with dramatically better benefits to employees all around America. I know this sounds too good to be true, but stay with me.

For me, it came down to puzzles and math.

I always hated puzzles. But what I realized during this journey was that it was like looking at an unfinished puzzle that had a number of big pieces missing. Then, to find out that these big missing pieces were many times *intentionally* left out of the puzzle, was just unnerving.

Then the math came into play.

I found out that fitting those missing pieces into place could save a company significant amounts of money. Each one of those missing pieces contained innovative brilliance. In fact, just putting one of those missing pieces into the puzzle could save a company anywhere from 10 to 15 percent. You put four of these big missing pieces back into the puzzle, and you've just saved a company between 40 to 60 percent on their healthcare.

What do these puzzle pieces look like? That's exactly what I will share with you in this book. But I need to tell you upfront, there are some old, rotten pieces of that puzzle that need to come out, and should never be used again.

Even though most of the content in this book is focused on positivity and exuberance, every business owner reading this book first has to realize why this topic of health insurance has been such an incredibly difficult nut to crack.

It is *extremely important* to understand what kind of hurdles stand in the way of businesses that want to achieve the same success others are realizing today.

Some of what you are about to read will certainly be disturbing.

The #1 Problem – A Rigged System

I'm going to start by explaining the number one problem that keeps employers from finding out about these transformative solutions. When you hear me explain this, you may be tempted to say to yourself, "that can't possibly be the number one problem with health insurance," but stick with me to the end of this before you draw any conclusions.

First, I want you to imagine a big hourglass. At the top of the hourglass, we'll put all of the employers around the country. No matter how big or how small, we'll put every employer that provides healthcare into the top section of this hourglass.

At the bottom of this hourglass, I want you to imagine every healthcare solution imaginable. This will include every insurance company, pharmacy company, hospital, primary-care doctor, out-patient surgery center, insurance network, and every other conceivable puzzle piece that encompasses our healthcare system. This will also include every Silicon Valley healthcare strategy and innovation that has come to the market within the last five to ten years.

Now imagine the narrow channel that slowly sifts the sand from the top section of the hourglass into the bottom section. We'll call this part "the distribution channel" for the sake of this discussion.

The only way for the sand to reach the bottom section of that hourglass is to travel through this channel. This metaphor is a good way for me to describe how most business owners make their decisions regarding which healthcare solution is best for them and their employees.

The trusted advisors who reside within these distribution channels are called brokers, and they work for different brokerage firms. Most of these brokerage firms form solid relationships with their employer clients. These employers look upon these firms as their access to all of the solutions at the bottom of the hourglass. Periodically, employers test the marketplace by shopping brokerage firms to see if there are solutions at the bottom of the hourglass that their current brokerage firm isn't offering.

Seems pretty logical and reasonable so far, right? Then why can virtually every employer relate to one of the following examples?

Example #1
Company of 20 Employees

Brokerage firm response: "Unfortunately. that's the best we can do."

You have been with the same insurance company for the past eight years. You naturally develop a comfortable and trusted relationship with most of your business vendors. You view your health-insurance company no differently. They have always paid your employees' claims on a timely basis, and your brokerage firm has even brought a representative from your insurance carrier along during the more difficult claims years. When your premiums have increased by as much as 20 to 40 percent, at least your broker (and the rep from the insurance company) were nice enough to sit down and negotiate a more reasonable increase.

The dramatic announcement of changing insurance carriers naturally makes your employees nervous about possibly losing their doctors or hospitals, so your broker usually recommends sticking with the same health-insurance company.

This always made sense. Don't rock the boat, but do the best you can to weather the storm. Your broker works hard for you, negotiates your increase down a few points—and he even worked with your HR director to get the newly negotiated rates ready for next year's payroll draw.

You get through the hard times, and during the more reasonable years (when your claims aren't so bad), you accept the smaller 6 to 8 percent increases and quickly get back to your business at hand.

One part of your strategy (devised by your broker) raised the deductibles for employees—adding a high-deductible health plan with an HSA element. In your employee meeting, you explain that rates are going up but that you are adding the HSA to help them out. You do your best to sell your employees on the concept of saving extra money from their payroll checks to contribute to their HSA accounts.

Later, you ask your broker if there isn't something different available in the marketplace because if the premiums keep going up while raising everyone's deductibles, this is simply going to be very difficult to manage. Your broker shrugs and says, "unfortunately, that's the best we can do."

Sound familiar?

Example #2
Company of 200 employees
$2,000,000 healthcare budget increasing
to $2,480,000 next year.

Broker's response: "Lucky we didn't get cancelled."

Your brokerage firm advised you two years ago to switch to a more reasonable-sounding coverage called a self-insured plan. This type of coverage allowed your company more control over your plan's overall costs. Instead of giving all of your money to the insurance company every year and never seeing a penny back, this was a way of paying claims out of your company's earnings and capping your financial exposure, in case some employees had high claims throughout the year. Your broker set things up so that your employees had the same network of doctors, hospitals, and pharmacy providers.

Most companies with 200 employees can have good-and bad-claims years. Yet statistically, those bad-claims years amount to only one or two out of every five years. During the good-claims years, you could potentially save a lot of money. The concept definitely made sense.

Then comes the really bad year, when, unfortunately, all hell breaks loose. Your $2,000,000 healthcare budget will go up to $2,480,000 in another three months. One employee of yours is receiving bone cancer treatments, and another employee had a premature baby and is still recovering in the hospital under 24/7 care. Then your brokerage firm comes back and tells you that no other self-insured stop-loss insurance carriers would even bid on your healthcare plan—so you have nowhere to go. You are stuck!

You tell your broker that you never intended to be in the insurance business—and isn't there another way to provide your employees decent healthcare without having the unforeseen claims of your employees forcing your prices up? He simply shrugs and says, "I think we just need to thank our lucky stars that our current insurance company didn't cancel us altogether."

Realizing no one else will even accept your offers, you suck it up and try to look forward with your best glass-half-full attitude. You increase your employees' share of their premiums and raise everyone's deductibles to soften the blow to your bottom line. Your employees don't really understand why their benefits are getting worse when most everyone else in the company is relatively healthy. You put the additional $480,000 into your operating-expense, but that means cutting back on all kinds of other things within your business.

Does this ring a bell?

Example #3
Company of 2,000 employees
Next year's healthcare budget is increasing
by an additional $1,000,000.

Brokerage firm's response: "We should at least feel good that you beat the benchmark."

You have sent your plan out for bid every three years with a request for proposal (RFP) to the biggest and best brokerage firms in your area. All of them seem to provide outstanding service for all of your HR team's needs, but now you need to explore some ideas on healthcare management. After all, this is the main reason for bringing other brokerage firms in every three to four years: healthcare is either your second- or third-biggest line item on your profit and loss statement each year. You may or may not attend these meetings as the CEO, but at least you make sure your leadership team is at these meetings to brainstorm any and all possible options in the marketplace. You have adopted seemingly sound wellness plans to keep your employees as healthy as possible, provided a broad level of insurance choices for the employees to satisfy every family's needs, and even provided the biggest national network available to accommodate your employees in all fifty states.

Since you have so many people on your plan (almost 4,200—with spouses and children), you know that self-insuring your plan still makes the most sense. At least, that's what your brokerage firm and your team are telling you.

Claims always seem to be an issue, though.

- Your budget for healthcare is now $20,000,000 each year and rising. Your leadership team tells you that in your self-insured plan, 85 percent of that figure (or

$17,000,000) is set aside within your company's checking account to pay the claims for all of your employees and their family members out of the earnings of your firm. The other $3,000,000 goes toward your fixed costs, consisting of insurance and administrative fees, which is awfully confusing.

- Your wellness plan is being offered to all of your employees, encouraging everyone to stop smoking, lose weight, exercise, and eat right. This wellness plan seems like an obvious no-brainer since healthier employees means fewer claims.

- Yet even with all of your healthcare management strategies, this has still brought you back to another increase of 7 percent.

- With a budget of $20,000,000 this year, that amounts to an extra $1,400,000 increase to your operating expenses next year.

Your benefits brokerage firm crunches the numbers with your team members and is ultimately able to reduce this 7 percent down to 5 percent. Your operating expenses now go up by $1,000,000 instead of $1,400,000. Your CFO has to feverishly go back to work to find other ways to reduce his numbers—cutting into other parts of your business is all he can do to make room for this massive increase for next year.

You try to calculate in your head how many additional new sales and after-tax revenue would be needed to make up for this enormous increase to your operating-expense budget.

When you ask your team members whether the brokerage firm foresees any new innovations that may be able to turn this ship around in future years, the answer is always the same. There is only so much they can do. They are circling back on your wellness programs and are going to redouble their efforts to encourage everyone to stay as healthy as possible. But at the end of the day, they say the claims are the claims.

Alert: Remember this phrase, *"The claims are the claims."*
The brokerage firm explains that you beat the benchmark of what other companies of your size and industry received in increases last year. On average, other companies similar to yours have received an average of 8 percent, so you should feel pretty good about your 5 percent.

And remember, you just went through an entire RFP process that took almost four months. You just got done pitting the "best-of-the-best" brokerage firms against each other. For now, this is the best you can do.

Is this feeling of swallowing hard and taking your lumps getting a little old?

Why does all of this keep happening?

The key is to understand how the major insurance companies, and their revenue streams, work behind the scenes. How they compensate their brokers and brokerage firms for selling their insurance products reveals a perverted system that rewards everyone but the employers and their employees. And the ever-increasing price of the actual healthcare for your employees has no limits on most employer plans. Our own government even passed a big law that made sure insurance company's contracts with employers had to provide "unlimited benefits" with no-caps for the costs of employee's healthcare.

Most people understand that if you buy insurance through an insurance agent, this insurance agent makes some kind of a commission selling this insurance. Yet, how this is all connected to insurance companies, brokers, and the brokerage firms is very misunderstood.

Every situation is a little different, but let me give you a little peek behind the scenes of how the hourglass situation actually plays out in the brokerage firm and health-insurance world.

My intention is to flip the hourglass upside down by the end of the book.

All of the proven solutions in the marketplace will be at the top of the hourglass for everyone reading this book to see. You will then be in control of choosing which is the best solution based upon your company's size and particular philosophy. Only after finding your proper solution will you look to get fitted with the proper solution partners, based on your particular choice in the marketplace.

Chapter two will reveal the *real stories* behind the three companies in examples #1, #2, and #3 from this first chapter. You may not get as angry as I did after finding out the real story behind these brokerage firm recommendations, but if it doesn't make you want to know more, you may have bought the wrong book.

The fact is that the average premiums for single employees are the equivalent of two or three car payments now. The average family premiums are equal two to three times most American's *mortgage payments*. Most employees would be unaware of this fact, since their employers pay a substantial portion of the employee's premiums, and sometimes (if they work for a larger company) even pay a good portion of their family premiums.

CHAPTER 2

MISALIGNED INCENTIVES AND HIDDEN REVENUE STREAMS

B rokerage firms don't get paid directly by you, the employer. Their revenues come in the form of either commissions from health-insurance carriers—or in other ways that I will explain shortly.

If they worked directly for you (the employer), you would receive a monthly invoice.

- Have you ever seen an invoice from a brokerage firm?
- Have you ever even thought to ask how they get paid or how much they get paid?

You will find out very soon that all of this is very intentional.

Let's look back at Example #1.

Years ago, your broker recommended that your 20-employee group choose one particular insurance company and stay with that company—which you've done for the last eight years. If your broker's commission was a percentage of what your company paid in premiums, your brokerage firm likely received an annual raise equal to the percentage your insurance premiums rose. This is not always the case in the small-group marketplace, but it is how a lot of plans are set up across America.

Let's assume your broker receives a 5 percent commission on your $200,000 annual premiums—or $10,000 a year. If your plan goes up 10 percent to $220,000, your brokerage firm will receive $11,000 in commissions the very next year. Not a lot, but it's still an extra $1,000 a year additional for your broker for simply renewing your plan with the same insurance company. If this broker has one hundred groups your same size, he will receive an additional $100,000 for helping his clients pay more, and to remain with the same insurance carrier.

Important Note: That 5 percent commission is a variable number chosen by the broker that is built into your healthcare contract. This percentage is usually within 3 to 10 percent of your annual premiums, based upon what the broker wants to put into the "commission section" box. This is usually listed in small print, somewhere at the bottom of a health insurance proposal. Most employers are unaware of what percentage their broker even receives each month. Some states have now adopted a per-employee per-month (PEPM) commission for brokers that range from $15 to $40 depending on which insurance company a broker chooses. Insurance companies now try to *entice* brokers to sell their products by offering higher PEPM's to their product lines.

Leaving your health insurance company the same requires the least amount of work for you and your HR team. No need to take extra time to shop the marketplace, compare prices and benefits, and no back-and-forth communications needed with your HR director. Most of the insurance company's networks overlap with each other nowadays, meaning your employees have little to no disruption regarding access to doctors and hospitals, should a broker recommend switching insurance providers.

By the way, leaving your coverage with the same insurance company requires almost zero work for your broker. In fact, if you keep your coverage with the same insurance carrier, your broker most times doesn't even need to tell your insurance provider that you are renewing. It all happens automatically these days. Unless you tell them otherwise, the carriers make the assumption that you are renewing your existing coverage and automatically send the new cards out to all of your employees. Easy Peasy.

Everyone keeps the same coverage, and employees automatically get their new cards in the mail. The only thing that changed was the cost went up 10 percent, and your broker got a little more in his or her pocket for next year. Out of sight, out of mind.

Not a lot of incentives built into this model for brokers or brokerage firms to work hard to lower your company's health insurance costs, are there?

Inside Information Fact:
Did you know that insurance companies also have something called "persistency bonuses"? These are massive bonuses paid out to brokers just for keeping the business with their particular favorite insurance carrier. And the reason many brokers

have their favorite insurance carriers is *because of these bonuses.*

Now think about where the incentives lie in a situation like this. Not only do the brokers and brokerage firms understand that reducing your total insurance costs would cause them to be paid less, but by also encouraging you to stay with the same insurance company, they are setting themselves up for huge bonuses at the end of each year.

When brokerage firms represent a company's health-insurance plan, they likely also represent all of the other benefits like your dental, life, disability, and even voluntary benefits that your employees purchase themselves. Of course, they also get paid commissions on these products as well. These commissions can amount to as much as 25-50 percent of what they make from their health-insurance commissions. A broker (in a case like this) may make as much as $13,000 to $17,000 a year from your company—*not including their big year-end bonuses.*

Remember, you never received an invoice from your brokerage firm. This is all paid out of commissions and bonuses from the insurance companies back to the brokers and their brokerage firms.

As an entrepreneur, I don't have a problem with companies making money, as long as the incentives are aligned properly and a company can demonstrate a clear value to the customer. But with incentives like these, is it any wonder that employers' healthcare costs have skyrocketed?

And this is anything but transparent!

Now, let's look back at Example #2

Remember, this is a company of 200 employees that is experiencing a difficult claims situation with two of their employees.

Maybe you're not a company that has faced this kind of dilemma, but it is actually not as uncommon as you would think.

Once again, are there financial incentives in place that could discourage a brokerage firm from looking to other solutions within the bottom of that hourglass? Let's have a look.

- If the brokerage firm was receiving commissions from the insurance carrier (or stop-loss insurance provider) and the rates went up, they received a raise.
- If your pharmacy benefit manager (PBM) raised their costs and your brokerage firm was paid a commission on this, they received an additional raise.
- And even though you're paying a third-party administrator (TPA) to manage your claims, do you know whether your brokerage firm gets compensated by them with "persistency bonuses" of some kind?

See what I mean?

But this particular situation in Example #2 has a twist. This broker was likely sweating bullets thinking that the insurance carrier might not just skyrocket their rates out of sight, but might drop them completely. Most brokers understand that companies face these kinds of issues periodically—and pray they get through it. Can you even imagine if your broker came back to you saying your current insurance carrier is cancelling your employee's insurance, and that no other insurance carrier will accept them?!

The truth is that solutions already exist today that forces insurance companies to accept situations just like this one. These solutions not only get employers out of terrible messes like this, but can actually save a company money. Most brokerage firms don't want you to know about these solutions, and if they even brought it up, they'd likely lose your business.

Sound too good to be true? Well, I'm here to tell you that it is very true.

I know of one company in my home state of Minnesota that had this very same dilemma. They transitioned their 150-employee firm to one of the "hidden from view" solutions presented in this book and actually saved over 50 percent in premiums. That amounted to a savings of $700,000 on their previous $1,300,000 in annual premiums. The company used much of this savings to reduce down the premiums for all employees. When asked at the employee meeting how everyone felt about this change, the employees broke out into a round of applause.

I knew the broker who orchestrated this change. He worked for one of the major brokerage firms in my area. I found out recently that he no longer works for this brokerage firm.

Why won't most brokerage firms sell these solutions? Because the fact is that brokerage firms make the most money selling the traditional retail plan or fully insured models. You know, the plans that continue to increase your premiums and decrease your benefits.

The unique program this broker used to save this company $700,000 paid about one-third the commissions and required ten times the amount of work. Since the financial incentives are misaligned, and most brokers are not prepared to work ten times harder, you will likely never be presented with the innovative solution described above. Hats off to this broker who went the extra mile. Most would not have gone down this road.

When you're counting on a broker or brokerage firm to show you all of the many solutions at the bottom of that hourglass, you will only see the ones they "want to show you" or "have the ability to show you."

Bottom line: they will usually protect their bottom line.

Finally, let's look back at Example #3.

You'd think that these larger companies of 2,000-plus employees are being shown every conceivable solution around the United States, and have done everything possible to fix their particular healthcare issues. Yet the same hourglass issue exists, whether it is a company of 20, 200, 2,000, or 20,000 employees. They are still only being shown the solutions that the brokerage firms choose to show them, rather than everything in the marketplace.

Why is this happening even up at 2,000- to 20,000-employee companies?

The short answer is that most brokerage firms choose to get you started off on the wrong foot.

The first thing most brokers do is to fit you with one of huge insurance carriers that seem to make everyone feel warm and fuzzy when they see these names on the employee's insurance cards. These major insurance carriers have seen their stock prices increase between 500 to 1200 percent since the passage of the Affordable Care Act in 2010. Each of these insurance carriers has affiliations with different "systems" that trap you into their spiderwebs.

The first trap is attaching your employees to their "PPO-discount" system. Under this system, the preferred-provider organizations (PPOs) give employees 30 to 50 percent discount-pricing for healthcare. What they don't tell the employers is that hospitals (and other healthcare providers) can charge outrageously high prices for procedures, and after applying these "wonderful discounts," the patients many times end up overpaying by anywhere from 200 to 2000 percent depending on which insurance carrier you have, which state you are in, and which hospital or healthcare provider you visit. In fact, hospitals many times have 100 to 150 different prices for performing the exact same procedure, in the exact same surgery room, within the exact same hospital. It just depends on which insurance carrier or contract was agreed to between their hospital chargemaster and the insurance company.

I dedicate a separate part of this book to address insurance networks and the backroom games being played at the expense of employers and employees. Most companies are never told that their network access is simply part of the spiderweb system that literally guarantees hospitals and healthcare providers can raise their prices in the future. It's easy to rent these networks through custom plan designs. But to truly impact the price of healthcare, companies are utilizing high-touch care navigator systems, and "bundle priced" healthcare providers from outside vendors. These vendors have negotiated prices with hospitals and providers inside each of these insurance networks. Employees can now get full knee replacements done for $16,000 to $22,000 through a bundled price vendor rather than be charged $45,000 to $65,000 after the nonsensical 50 percent discount from a $90,000 to $130,000 hospital chargemaster price handed down from on high.

By simply utilizing one of the many high-touch care navigator vendors, an employee can just call the phone number on their insurance card and be directed to a higher-quality, lower-cost provider for their knee-replacement surgery. For simply utilizing this simple but effective care navigator system, the employer can reward the employee by wiping out their deductibles and out-of-pocket costs completely. This is just one of the many innovations that are revolutionizing the employer-employee healthcare world. The employee still has the choice of using the PPO-network system, but would pay their normal deductibles of $3000 to $6000, and their out-of-pocket maximums of $8000 to $16,000. And who would do that when your employer allows you an alternative at $0 cost to you with the same or better healthcare outcomes?

One of the other sinister traps that the insurance companies do is to attach themselves (and your company) to one of the "Big-Three" Pharmacy Benefit Managers (PBMs). These three PBMs control almost 80 percent of the entire United States employer marketplace. If you are using one of these PBMs, you are likely being overcharged by approximately 40 to 70 percent. Most companies don't even know who their pharmacy benefit managers are, let alone how they operate within "the system." These three PBM's have dozens of different ways to hide their revenue streams from public view. You've heard of "Big Pharma?" These are the primary ones that they're talking about. The good news is that there are many other fiduciary-responsible PBMs that companies can utilize to quickly reduce pharmacy expenditures in as little as 90-120 days. But the big insurance carriers (and many times the brokerage firms) don't want you to switch to any of these other PBMs because of their cozy revenue relationships with the "big three monopoly." When employers realize these big savings by switching PBM's, the employers can then afford to give employees zero-dollar copays for their much-needed maintenance medications. Employers save. Employees save. A win-win for all.

The story remains the same though:

1. The revenue incentives between brokerage firms and insurance companies are completely misaligned with the employer's needs and desires.
2. How the brokerage firms get compensated, even up at these high levels, is still being hidden from employers.
3. The brokers working for these big brokerage firms are simply "working within the system" and have little-to-no say regarding these revenue arrangements.
4. Since the brokers are getting paid handsomely by working within the system, they are more than happy to keep quiet about these arrangements. Many times, the brokers can be blind to these arrangements. After all, they didn't invent the system—they are only working "within the system."

I'm not telling you today that your own broker is *for sure* getting all of these "behind-the-scenes" revenues from these different sources. But hopefully, this will at least spark an inquiry if you've been unaware of any of these things up until now. As of the writing of this book, recent regulation has passed requiring brokerage firms and insurance companies to reveal all revenue sources to the public. This *may be* a huge breakthrough in the marketplace. We'll see how all of this plays out. The way I understand this legislation, the brokers and brokerage firms still won't pay any penalties for having these arrangements.

The fact is, there are fees for so many things within a self-insured plan design that it is seriously difficult to keep track of it all. And which parts of the plan are helping your company, and which ones are not, is a whole other topic. For instance, there is usually a sizeable fee paid to a brokerage firm for any wellness program you may be using. Did you know that wellness programs have been statistically proven to produce $0.00 ROI for all of their purported efforts? This has been true for decades.

Hidden revenues are one thing. But remember that phrase "the claims are the claims"?

The company of 2,000 employees in Example #3 was paying its claims out of that big $17,000,000 pool of money, which is the earnings of the company. Wouldn't it make sense for someone to have a plan to make sure that that money was spent wisely on behalf of all of those employees and their family members each year? It is true that claims are going to happen, and that people still need to be cared for properly when these claims occur, but leaving this up to an insurance company to "figure this out for you and your employees" is like leaving the fox in charge of the hen house. To trust that money to anyone that tells you "the claims are the claims" is not only irresponsible—it is bordering on criminal.

The incredible 21st century innovative solution partners that are being hidden from view by that narrow "distribution channel" have already figured out different ways to impact the number, size, and frequency of your employees' claims—sometimes so dramatically that they have reduced these internal costs by 40 to 60 percent *with better medical outcomes*.

Now that's real healthcare! And that's also real money, folks!

Again, I have no problem with companies making money in the marketplace—as long as they are transparent with their fees and are clearly providing value to the customer.

Yet many times, employers are being kept in the dark about the many choices within the bottom of that solution-filled hourglass simply because of misaligned incentives and hidden-revenue arrangements.

Let me give you a sense of what is hidden from view at the bottom of that hourglass for midsize to larger companies.

Everyone understands how technology has advanced just about every other part of our lives. Most don't understand how technology has advanced the healthcare industry for employers.

The digital-health industry is booming like never before in America. In fact, in 2019, so much venture capital money went into the digital-health industry that it exceeded the three previous years of 2016, 2017, and 2018 *combined*. This technology is specifically designed to control the number, size, and frequency of claims within a self-insured plan for companies all the way down to 125 employees. Most of these digital-health solutions will immediately reduce an employer's costs by 15-20 percent in the very first year. For the company we were talking about in Example #3, this would have meant a reduction of $3,000,000 in the first year—instead of a $1,000,000 increase.

Because most brokerage firms have misaligned financial incentives, thanks to their cozy insurance-company relationships, their customers will likely never be presented with any kind of digital-health solutions whatsoever.

The good news is that large companies like these can now have no-cost audits done by independent healthcare consulting groups. This will not only tip the hourglass upside down and reveal all of the innovative solutions available to them all around the United States, but will also provide claims-analysis comparisons that will give employers a chance to see just what kind of savings they could have achieved in previous years, compared to what they have been doing within their current programs.

These audits can even uncover previous revenue-sharing arrangements that employers couldn't possibly have known about from their current brokerage firms. As you can imagine, many times this information is not met with a lot of friendly cooperation from insurance carriers or brokerage firms.

Yet most CEOs or CFOs would know this much:

If any vendor is truly looking out for a company's best interests, they shouldn't be afraid of these types of transparent audits.

Let me be very clear about something else at this point.

Brokerage firms *are an extremely valuable resource* for any employer offering benefits to their employees. In fact, I devote an entire chapter in this book to the enormous value that brokerage firms bring to employers. Brokerage firms provide many other things besides healthcare for businesses. When you list out all of the many benefits that brokerage firms manage, it is a very, very long list. Beyond health insurance, a brokerage firm might manage a company's dental, life, disability, HSA, flex-spending account, workers compensation, 401(k), coordination with payroll, and the list goes on and on from there.

It is not my intention to tell any business owner that they can manage all of these benefits without the assistance of a competent brokerage firm. My point is that with all of these many benefits being managed for an employer, how much attention is really being given to a company's healthcare management? The market is crying out for specialists in this area. Especially since the costs of healthcare can eat up 60 to 80 percent of a company's total employee-benefit budget each and every year.

Every business needs a real "check under the hood" once in a while, in any part of their business, to make sure everything is running the way it's supposed to run. Auditing this part of a business can produce some dramatic results when done properly.

The bottom line is, brokerage firms are spread too thin. On top of that, most brokerage firms are operating within a system that aligns their interests with insurance companies and pharmacy firms, not the employers (and their employees) that pay all the bills and premiums.

Once I found out how to peel back the *Wizard of Oz* curtain and reveal what's really going on behind the scenes, it truly lit a fire within me. This is one of the main reasons why I wrote this book.

Milton Friedman, an American economist, used to say, "the world runs on individuals pursuing their separate interests."

It's extremely important to ask yourself: "Who is looking out for my company and my best interests within the area of my business healthcare?"

I am a huge fan of the underdogs of this world—I see the employers and their employees as huge underdogs who have been beaten down because of this nonsense for decades now. In fact, most employees are completely unaware of how health insurance even works—and why all of this is happening to them.

It's the *employees* of all of these companies that I am fighting for more than anyone else. They are the main reason I wrote this book!

Remember what I said in the first chapter of this book, that employees around the country are actually going bankrupt even when they have health insurance. That is unacceptable!

This is what truly brings out my anger and frustration relating to this issue. I have allowed this anger to propel me over the last six years toward finding solutions—and I am now ready to bring these outstanding innovations and solutions to businesses and their employees across America.

Waiting on the "other side" for the readers of this book are:

- Big savings for employers,
- Zero-deductible health plans and lower premiums for employees, and
- Control over business-healthcare costs for every size business once and for all.

Imagine standing up at your next open-enrollment meeting and telling your employees their insurance premiums are going down—and their health benefits are going up.

Have they *ever* heard those words before?

Health insurance may suck right now, my friends—but not for long.

CHAPTER 3

HOW THE HELL DOES HEALTH INSURANCE EVEN WORK?

T he short answer is obvious—it doesn't! But this is such a complicated subject that I find most people get confused about even the definitions of health insurance and healthcare. So, let's look at two questions:

- What is health insurance, and how does it work?
- What is healthcare, and how does it work?

It is *really important* that I first give you a general understanding of how *health insurance* actually works. The good news is, it doesn't have to be as difficult as most people make it out to be.

Imagine that you lived in a small town of a thousand people. At the town hall meeting, all of you decide to chip in $100 a month to help out everyone in the town with the costs for their healthcare. The town's treasurer takes everyone's payment and deposits that money at the local bank. This big pool of money is available to cover any medical bills that the townspeople incur over a certain amount (let's say $500 per person per year). The bank is nice enough to add an additional line of credit in case claims go over the $1,200,000 combined deposit that the town makes each year.

Next, the treasurer hires an extremely responsible administrator to distribute the money as needed to the local healthcare providers when there's a claim. The administrator keeps careful records of all the transactions and provides a monthly report to the treasurer. Both the administrator and the treasurer make sure they never overpay for services—because they signed a contract of fiduciary or financial responsibility to the townspeople. It's their responsibility that no one gets overcharged, double-billed, or that anything else unethical is done. In essence, they have a legal responsibility and they know they can be audited at any time.

Now, say someone breaks his ankle. He is taken to the hospital, where the doctor sets the broken ankle and puts him in a cast. The hospital charges are carefully reviewed by the watchdog administrator. He determines that a fair and reasonable price was charged by all, as he had set up an agreed-upon price system with all the hospitals and healthcare providers in the area. In this case, the hospital receives a payment of $1,750 and the doctor receives a payment of $1,250, for a total charge of $3,000. The patient has to pay only the first $500; the administrator pays out the other $2,500 to the doctor and the hospital, and the transaction is complete.

Seems pretty simple, right?!

Each and every year, $1,200,000 goes into the bank from the one-thousand residents in the town. Some years, claims could go over that amount, but most years, the town stays well under its budget. It usually ends up running a surplus, and no individual resident pays out any more than $500 per medical occurrence at any time. The town's people may even vote to use some of their surplus money to help the more-needy people within their community. Everyone's happy and secure, and the town's residents have all of their healthcare covered.

Even though I didn't use the term "health insurance" one time, this little story gives us a simple model to understand even a complex insurance system.

Every health-insurance program in America consists of the exact same elements:

- Claims
- Reserves
- Administration
- Pooling charges (or stop-loss insurance coverage)

Many acronyms exist in this business, but this is my favorite one: CRAP.

If you are an employer covering your employees through any of the major insurance carriers around the nation, this is how the insurance companies break down the costs within your plan:

- 80 to 85 percent of your premium dollars go toward paying claims.
- The rest of the 15 to 20 percent goes toward the reserves, administration, and pooling costs.

Most employers do not understand the pooling-cost element of their plans.

Understanding "Pooling Charge"

A pooling charge is an internal cost charged by the insurance company to offload any claims above a certain amount. For instance, if you are covered under a traditional group health plan, it would pay any of the claims, for any one individual, up to that pooling point (let's say that pooling point amount is $50,000). If any one person's claim exceeds that $50,000, the insurance company offloads that risk to a separate insurance provider. These are called stop-loss insurance companies. Each pooling point is different, but if you think your insurance company is taking on all of the risk for all of the members within your business, you are sadly mistaken. Insurance is a very shrewd business, and they would not take on unnecessary risks.

Fully-insured or "retail plans" as I will be calling them in this book, give the insurance companies total control over your money and charge you a monthly amount in the form of premiums. These retail-plan premiums give employers no chance of recovering a single dime of their own money once it is in the hands of the insurance companies.

Companies around the nation are finally recognizing the value of using custom health plan designs to their advantage. In fact, as of 2020, over 60 percent of employers are choosing custom-designed health plans over the traditional retail plans. The simple reason is that custom health plans allow the employer to hang on to most of their own money.

- If you are a company of one hundred employees, you are likely spending around $1,000,000 each year.
- 80 percent of this money ($800,000) goes to paying claims, and 20 percent ($200,000) goes into the reserves, administration, and pooling costs (we call these collective costs *fixed costs* within the industry).
- The custom health-plan strategy is: "Why not have your own company pay these claims costs, and save money during the good years when you have lower-than-expected overall claims?"

Now, I don't want you to go completely crazy on me at this point. Most people tend to freak out at the thought of "paying their own claims." It's normal to think that you might have a high claim and have to pay out an enormous amount of money in a particular month. In fact, systems are already in place to make sure that this can never happen. This is why I wanted to explain the pooling charge (or stop-loss insurance) that protects you in the case of any large claims that occur. When you set up your own custom design, you choose your own "pooling point" and purchase your own stop-loss insurance coverage. You also choose your own third-party administrator (TPA) to process everyone's claims, and then simply choose a proper pharmacy benefit manager (PBM) to coordinate with your TPA to pay all pharmacy costs. Now that wasn't so hard, was it?

Custom plans have been in place for a long time, but in recent years they have stepped-up in a really big way. There are plans out there that allow you to still pay a "guaranteed-level amount" (the same as your retail plan model), and if you don't burn through all of your claims pool money, you keep it in your business. Don't let a broker scare you away from a custom plan model. It likely means this broker either doesn't understand these systems, or they are scared of losing your business to someone else who does.

It has been proven over time that, statistically, you will likely have a bad claims experience about one or two years out of every five. Hanging on to some of that $800,000 every year and controlling how that money is being spent can mean a significant amount of savings for a small company of 100 employees.

The most significant innovations and changes over the last decade have come in the form of controlling *how those claims dollars are being spent.* Whether you are a company of 100, 1,000, or 100,000 employees, getting a handle on the number, size, and frequency of these claims is critical. There are even plans that allow you to price your own healthcare now. I know that sounds a little nutty on the surface, but these plans have specific prices for every conceivable healthcare situation in the marketplace. In other words, you decide (as an employer) what the healthcare prices will be for any of your employees and their dependents ahead of time. When executed properly, these types of designs save anywhere from 30-60 percent when compared to a retail plan design.

Approximately 157 million individuals around the United States are insured through their employers. Believe it or not, 85 percent of these people (that's right, nearly 133.5 million individuals) are employed by small to mid-size businesses These smaller sized businesses have been crushed by the enormous increases over the last several decades by health-insurance costs increasing year after year. Sometimes these increases have averaged as much as 6 to 8 percent a year for companies that have experienced higher than expected claims. Providing health insurance to employees has become a massive financial burden for these organizations—but it's also a necessity. In order to compete with other companies in the marketplace to attract and retain top talent, they feel like they *must* offer health insurance.

However, the drastic increases in health-insurance costs aren't only affecting the companies' bottom lines. Most times, the employees share in the cost of these health-insurance premiums. This lowers their incomes, as higher percentages are withheld from their paychecks each and every year. In fact, some studies have shown that close to 70 percent of employees didn't receive the raises they so richly deserved over the last twenty years, primarily because most of that money went toward health-insurance premium increases.

Nobody seems to fully understand the reasoning behind these extreme increases over the years, but specific incidents and government mandates have certainly paved the way toward this destruction. Frankly, most of the brokers around the country don't even understand it in its entirety—and they are the ones representing the insurance companies!

I was one of those brokers, and for the last twenty-four years, I have dealt with these increases first-hand. Despite every effort to advocate for my employer clients, when it came time for them to renew their healthcare coverage, I would be delivering news of increases sometimes as high as 30 to 40 percent.

Like most other brokers, I thought that the best I could do was to request quotes from the other insurance carriers available to my clients. If I were lucky, I would get a quote that would drop their annual increase down by 10 to 15 percent. But, if the rate increase by their previous insurance provider was 30 percent, switching insurance companies to save 10 percent would still leave my clients with a 20 percent increase.

For decades, I really thought that was the best I could do for my clients. Sadly, as I stated earlier, I came to realize that I was simply a part of the problem.

What is healthcare and how does this work?

The short answer is, there has never truly been any system designed to contain what hospitals and other healthcare providers can charge for their healthcare services. I can tell you right now that this dirty little game is coming to an end, and quicker than you think!

Many businesses are waking up to this crazy health-insurance/risk management game. They are realizing that there are ways of providing money directly to their employees, allowing *them* to purchase, own, and design their own coverage, and get out of having a "mini-insurance company" within their business.

Remember when retirement plans started switching from pension plans to 401k's? This was a relatively simple concept that is now playing out in the business healthcare world. It made sense in the pension/401k space to have employees own their own contracts, rather than employers, from a basic macro-economic point of view. Why should employers control the money invested for their employees, and take on all that extra risk and responsibility? I remember the naysayers saying "this will never work." Well look at where we are at today. It turns out employees are happier making their own decisions for themselves and their families owning their own 401k plans. Imagine that?!
The employer now allows all employees to contribute what they want, and most times the employer includes a matching contribution. How does shifting employers from owning healthcare contracts to their employees change the game within this crazy mixed-up industry? Stay tuned.

CHAPTER 4

THE OVERRIDING PROBLEM—AND
THE ONE-WORD SOLUTION!

Years ago, I put together a survey that I sent to all of my business-owner clients who had health insurance for their employees. In short, I wanted to know what they would like to see different from their healthcare plans. The answers varied, ranging from specifics surrounding deductibles, copays, and networks, to angry complaints about costs. But one of the responses was right on point, summarizing what everyone else was trying to say in two simple words:

"Better – Cheaper."

At the time, I thought it was hilarious, not only because of his short two-word response, but I also considered it an absolute impossibility in this age of complicated and highly regulated healthcare. It went against the trends of skyrocketing annual premiums, as well as the deterioration in the quality of healthcare benefits.

After almost six years of research and investigation into the topic, I discovered that it's not an impossibility. Believe it or not, I found out that "Better - Cheaper" already exists today!

Yet, we must first seek to truly understand the problems in healthcare before evaluating the solutions.

Let's examine each of the main problems a bit deeper.

The Overriding Problems

There are three main problems with health insurance: it's complicated and expensive, it has led to feelings of helplessness and apathy, and decisions on health insurance only happen once a year.

1. It's Complicated and Expensive.

Chances are that you are fully aware that health insurance is already ridiculously expensive. But have you ever stopped to consider the reasons why or where all of that money goes?

Most people don't even understand the language associated with health insurance, let alone the bigger picture of why costs are skyrocketing. In fact, many feel *the reason it is so expensive is because it's so complicated.* To a significant extent, they're right.

Very few employers have actually taken the time to dig deep and determine why their insurance is costing them what it does. Maybe they have even found some less-expensive options for themselves—but they rarely get to the heart of the problem.

And with so many moving parts, is it any wonder why the complications of health insurance overwhelm most people? Most businesses don't have the time or the resources to explore every aspect of healthcare.

The sad truth is that many within the industry *are using the complications* to hide the already-existing solutions from employers. They are making a killing because of employers' lack of knowledge.

2. We Feel Helpless.

Even the small segment of folks who do understand why their insurance is eating into so much of their incomes every month have come to accept it as a painful necessity. We've come to believe that American health insurance is a lost cause that can't be improved. As a nation, we feel helpless knowing it is something we can't live with and can't live without. Accepting something as destructive as this is unacceptable to me. I don't blame employers for feeling apathetic over this subject. But for employers today, I look at this situation the same as the age-old joke about the psychologist and the light bulb.

How many psychologists does it take to change a light bulb? One, but the light bulb "has to want to change."

For employers that truly want something different, the answers are better today than ever before. But, once you read about the alternatives within this short book, it's truly up to you to take action towards adopting and implementing the solution that fits your business.

3. We Set it and Forget it.

For most people, once a year—and only once a year—a decision on health insurance is made. The fate of their healthcare is solidified within a plan that is determined by either the employer or the individual (depending on who owns the health-insurance contract)—and it's chosen as if it were simply another ugly task to mark off a "things-to-do" list.

This decision comes into our field of vision only annually, and when that plan is set and the paperwork is signed, it is quickly removed from our minds. It's easy to forget about it because the money is usually automatically deducted from a company's business account, as well as automatically deducted from the employees' paychecks. The costs are hidden from view, softening the blow.

The Undeniable Solution

Here's the good news. I have discovered the one-word solution to the healthcare and health-insurance problem in this country: freedom.

Freedom, by my definition, is "the ability to act without forcible restraint by others."

Most people understand that individual freedom is important. Living in a country that allows people the freedom to do as they please can be a wonderful thing. In fact, most Americans take this for granted. But if you ever want to know who really appreciates this freedom, ask anyone who has lived in a different country where governments and dictators made all the rules for them. Remember those people standing at the Berlin Wall in Germany after the Soviet Union collapsed? People were reaching up from the east side of the wall—and being pulled up to freedom on the west side. Can you imagine what it must have felt like, literally being lifted to freedom? These people hold a much deeper connection and appreciation for their personal freedoms. They treasure their freedom and are truly grateful for all that it provides.

Economic Freedom

While individual freedom brings about deep emotions for many people, most people don't completely understand the concept of *economic freedom*. Economic freedom deals with businesses and individuals trying to avoid the barrage of rules and regulations imposed by everyone from federal and state governments, to unions, insurance companies, and any other large institutions that restrict pure innovation. The health-insurance industry has to deal with all of this and much more. In fact, the health-insurance companies impose so many rules that many times, a company can't even qualify for coverage due to their participation requirements. Imagine wanting to provide healthcare for your employees—and the rules state that you can't even buy it. How ridiculous is that?! You'll find out an incredibly simple way to avoid this ridiculous "participation rule" in the subsequent chapters of this book.

When you combine political freedom with economic freedom, you literally have the fundamental solution to almost any problem for any sector of our economy. This combination of freedom can solve issues in our educational system, quickly advance technology, lower energy prices, and yes, it can even solve healthcare.

When this kind of freedom truly exists, it increases choice and competition within every sector of the marketplace. Choice and competition drive prices down and improves the quality of products and services.

When people and businesses are completely free to innovate and compete, the sky's the limit on what can be achieved.

Businesses, both small and large, have newfound freedoms in healthcare today that they haven't had in decades. This is due in large part to recent legislation passed in June of 2019, which went into effect on January 1, 2020. Most all of the penalties are gone for individuals and businesses regarding the health-insurance rules of the Affordable Care Act or Obamacare. This allows businesses and individuals many more choices and innovative opportunities than ever before.

Unfortunately, most businesses are still operating from the traditional practice of fighting against premium and deductible increases for their employees under the old systems. A new trend is on the rise, though. It's one of lower premiums and better benefits. If you think this all sounds like a too-good-to-be-true scenario, you're not alone. That's exactly what I thought when I heard about it initially. Lower premiums with better benefits? C'mon?!

It is true, though. Many of the solutions are new and improved as of 2020—and I'll describe the best of them in this book.

I no longer operate in the role of a broker. I have realized a deeper responsibility of being a facilitator of this newfound information. My goal is to spread the good word about this movement around the country to ensure others have the opportunity to take advantage of these savings for themselves. I want employers big and small to realize they can once again offer decent healthcare that doesn't break the bank for employers—and particularly for their employees.

My new role is as a super-connecter. My mission is to fast-track businesses of all sizes into the hands of the highest-level solution partners around the country. The most complicated part is identifying which hidden solution is right for which company. If you are a company of 5 to 50 employees, there are a few common-sense solutions available to a company your size. If you are a company of 50 to 500 employees, there is a completely different set of solutions available to you. Companies of 500 to 5000 employees have an even greater set of opportunities. And companies of 5000 to 100,000 employees enjoy the top-level choices.

You may be asking yourself, "Why aren't all solutions available to companies of all sizes?" This is an extremely good question, and, oddly enough, it has a simple answer. Not all solution partners make themselves available to just any size company in the marketplace.

One of the premier Silicon Valley companies on the west coast, only offers its services to companies' of 1000 employees or more. Since this company only started up eight years ago, they only offer their services in sixteen states so far. Another plug and play digital solution offers its services in all fifty states but focuses most of their marketing to 5000 employees and up. I am also connected to about two hundred top-level consultants around the country. Many of these consultants even own and run their own brokerage firms. They choose to incorporate the "service side" of the industry and try to manage all of the employee benefits for their clients. Every one of these consultants has a different niche in the marketplace. Some of them will only consult on companies that are 50 to 500 employees. Others focus on the small market of 2- to 50-employee companies. Trying to determine which is the right fit for your company, in your industry, at your size is a very time-consuming task. All I am trying to do as a super-connector is to fast-track employers into the hands of the best people (and solution partners) that match up with your particular philosophy.

It all starts with uncovering the hidden solution partners behind the Wizard of Oz curtain. Once an employer has a chance to see these hidden solutions, they can decide which philosophy fits them best. After that, just match up the best solution partners, consultants, and even brokerage firms to help execute your particular program.

Regardless of the size of your company, real freedom exists in the business-healthcare space in 2020 and beyond. Cutting through the red tape of rules and regulations and getting businesses positioned to operate from a place of real freedom takes careful deliberation.

This book will provide you with three very important things:

- Knowledge
- Access
- Execution

The most important of all of these is knowledge. Once you have the knowledge and have carefully deliberated as to which "freedom solution" is right for your business, companies all around America are ready and willing to help you with access and execution. They get paid for helping businesses save money and deliver better benefits for you and your employees.

Most brokers, brokerage firms, and insurance companies don't want you to gain knowledge about these freedom-fighting solution partners in the marketplace. They only want you to see "their solutions" at the bottom of that hourglass.

In other words, we are tipping the hourglass—and the entire health-insurance industry—upside down.

CHAPTER 5

NEW REVELATIONS

My First Eye-Opening Moment

The first moment when I realized what was wrong with American healthcare—and what the cure was—came about six years ago when I read the book The CEO's Guide to Restoring the American Dream by Dave Chase. In this book, he reveals the many layers of corruption that exist within our system of healthcare. Hospitals, pharmacy companies, insurance companies, brokers, and brokerage firms are all adding to the problems within the healthcare and health-insurance industry.

Dave Chase leads an organization called The Health Rosetta. You can find them at www.healthrosetta.org. This is the only structured organization that I am aware of that is thoroughly committed to reducing down the entire cost of healthcare nationwide. His concept is simple: reduce the cost of healthcare and it will reduce the cost of health insurance.

Many players have their hands in the cookie jar. They are all benefiting from a system that hides behind an unending maze of complexities that cause most reasonable people to throw up their hands in disgust and give up on the whole mess.

Instead of focusing on those negatives, however, my goal in this book is to focus on the positive: finding the new freedoms within the system.

Free-market custom health-plan designs are already sweeping the nation for larger companies. The larger the company, the more leverage they have in the marketplace. If you have enough employees, you naturally have a lot of clout because everyone wants your business. But the big-company solutions of yesterday are now available to much-smaller companies around the USA today.

Years ago, a consultant by the name of Tom Emerick helped Walmart develop an extremely successful Center of Excellence (COE) program. This program brought the best-of-the-best to the forefront for all major life-threatening surgical events. Tom searched all around the USA to find teams of doctors who were the most successful in their particular fields at treating major life-threatening events. Since these complicated, high-cost surgeries comprised the lion's share of Walmart's claims, it made sense for him to focus on controlling these huge costs. His journey not only took him to places of healthcare excellence, but also to the realization that by utilizing these Rockstar medical centers, costs were lower—a lot lower. Did you know that almost 30 percent of cancers are misdiagnosed around the United States? Neither did I!

In a recent study, 88 percent of patients who visited one of their smart-care centers at the Mayo Clinic received a new or refined diagnosis. Walmart was able to improve the ultimate health outcomes of its employees while lowering its overall cost of healthcare spending.

Walmart went on to establish these smart-care medical centers all around the United States, bringing outstanding results to heart surgeries, transplant surgeries, cancer treatments, and complex spine procedures. Since the outcomes were better and the costs were lower overall, a Walmart employee could utilize the benefits of Tom's program and pay $0.00 out-of-pocket—a win-win for both employer and employee.

This one program reduced Walmart's $6 billion annual spending by $1.8 billion in eighteen months (and has kept it down ever since). Walmart has now signed off on Tom Emerick's program, and allowed Tom to offer this same Center of Excellence program through his new company, Edison Healthcare. This same program is now available to any company with more than 750 employees all around the country. Recognize the freedom?

Another newfound freedom can be found in the area of the pharmacy industry. As I mentioned before, there are three PBM's (pharmacy benefit managers) that have monopolized the employer-sponsored healthcare space across America. Their specialty is leveraging the insurance company's third-party payer system—and hiding revenue streams within their models. Most employers don't even know that they have one of these big-three PBMs within their retail-health-plan designs. This is worth mentioning again, because this is one of the easiest fixes within an employer healthcare plan. In the industry we call this the "low hanging fruit" due to the simplicity of making this one simple change for an employer.

The good news? Employers are now free to choose a wide variety of fiduciary-responsible pharmacy benefit managers from all around the country for their custom health plan designs. Replacing one of these big-three PBMs with a fiduciary-responsible PBM can reduce employers' pharmacy costs by 40 to 70 percent within 90 days. Essentially, these fiduciary-responsible PBMs choose to source their prescription purchases at wholesale prices rather than retail prices.

They still make a small profit on every drug they represent, but it is completely transparent to the employer (consumer). They produce the same drugs, using the exact same delivery systems—at half the costs. Your employees can use the exact same drug stores and use the same delivery methods of receiving their drugs. The employers, as well as their employees, get the advantage of the huge savings. Many employers that have switched to this model are eliminating co-pays for their employees. This is a far cry from many Americans splitting pills in half just to make their drugs more affordable under America's retail plan system. It is absolutely appalling.

It's easy to recognize this new freedom of course. The employees notice it right away.

Out-patient surgery centers are also stepping up all over America. The Surgery Center of Oklahoma is leading the way. Charging a fraction of what hospitals charge, Dr. Keith Smith's Surgery Center of Oklahoma has been in business well over twenty years. They haven't raised their prices once over that entire time. In fact, they have actually lowered their prices three times! You can see all of their prices on drop-down menus right on their website. I recently looked up a full knee replacement and saw it was $15,499. Ask around town to see what your local hospitals and other providers might charge for a full knee replacement. It could be $140,000 at one place and $70,000 at another facility across town. In fact, it could be that you can find that same discrepancy *within the same hospital*. One PPO-health-insurance network might have one price, while the next

PPO network provides another. Don't be surprised if they tell you to check with your insurance company about the price of your knee replacement when you go into your healthcare provider or hospital. This response still ticks me off!

Employers that have access to Oklahoma's Surgery Center (through an employer's custom health plan design) can have an employee (and spouse) flown down to Oklahoma, have the surgery performed, and have them flown back at $0.00 cost to the employee. Most employers pay the entire cost of the flights and hotels as well.

Now that's what I call freedom and innovation!

Direct Primary Care (DPC)

Direct Primary Care (DPC) services are also becoming commonplace in the marketplace. DPC doctors are doctors that operate outside of the crazy insurance-industry mess. They are free to operate as they please and avoid the massive amounts of administrative hassles associated with insurance companies.

I had my own personal experience with a DPC doctor here in my home state of Minnesota. I was interviewing a doctor that operated out of Minneapolis. He was visiting with me regarding a client of mine that currently was considering a custom health plan, and was looking to offer his DPC services to all of their 137 employees and their families. For a set amount per employee per month, the doctor offered unlimited visits and even made house calls like the old days. Remember the show Marcus Welby MD? If you don't, you can google it. Old folks like me remember him well.

This DPC doctor told me that he gets wholesale pricing on a long list of generic medications. Most of these medications he just passes through to the consumer because he doesn't want (or need) to make any money off of those.

The concept goes like this. The employer would pay the entire cost of the doctor's normal monthly subscription fee of $30-$50 per month for single employees and $70-$90 a month for families. The employees would have the option of either seeing this DPC doctor at no cost, or seeing their regular doctors for the usual $50 to $150 office visit copays.

The DPC doctor not only offers great savings on prescription drugs, but also provides direct connections to reduced pricing for imaging services such as MRIs, X-rays, CT scans, and other services. As I continued to talk with him, I started thinking to myself, "Why wouldn't I consider using this guy"? So, I signed up for his DPC service for both my wife and myself.

I recently was having a minor shoulder problem. I had received two cortisone shots over the past six months that had cost me $200 each time I went in, *and I had paid the cash price* at my orthopedics' office. My new DPC doctor came to see me at my home, did a two-hour evaluation of my complete medical history, and while he was there administered another cortisone shot. This was only one week after I signed up for his service. He sent me an email with the bill about two days later for the cortisone shot—for $11.00. He explained to me that even though I paid cash at my orthopedics' office, they still mark it up anywhere from 1000 to 2000 percent. I am now getting my maintenance medications for next to nothing and was left wondering, "Why didn't I look into this sooner for me and my wife?"

Thanks to technological advances (along with the recent spread of COVID-19), more and more DPC services are now available online. Apps allow almost any size employer to connect employees to DPC nurses and doctors via their smartphones. These nurses and doctors can authorize prescriptions right over the phone and provide a "concierge-like" service for employees. This is a true game-changer.

Hospitals and PPO Networks

Hospital costs are an entirely different animal. President Trump has recently signed an executive order requiring hospitals to be transparent in their pricing. This may be one of the boldest moves by the federal government in the history of healthcare.

The Department of Health and Human Services has announced that the Centers for Medicare & Medicaid Services (CMS) is issuing two rules that take historic steps to increase price transparency to empower patients and increase competition among all hospitals, group health plans, and health-insurance issuers in the individual and group markets. These prices have been out of control for decades.

Hospitals have hidden their price and cost structures within the insurance company's PPO networks to their advantage in the most sinister way.

Let me give you a little sneak peek behind the scenes of something called the "hospital chargemaster." The hospital chargemaster utilizes the insurance company's "PPO discounts" to hide the real costs of their procedures.

Let's use the same full knee replacement surgery that I mentioned before. One hospital attached to one insurance-company PPO may give a hospital chargemaster price of $140,000. When the patient applies their 50 percent PPO discount, they only get charged $70,000 for that surgery. Another hospital attached to a different PPO-insurance-company network may charge $80,000 for that same knee replacement surgery, apply a 50 percent discount, and ultimately charge the patient $40,000 for the same service. The issue is not the size of the discount from the PPO, the issue is that the "hospital chargemaster" can put almost any price they want into the cost of that full knee replacement. One hospital charge is $140,000 and another charge is $80,000, and no one even knows. Worse yet, most don't even care!

Red Flag: Did you know that some insurance companies now own hospital systems? Did you also know that some hospital systems own some insurance companies? Interesting huh?!

Meanwhile, we already know that The Surgery Center of Oklahoma charges $15,499.00 for a full knee replacement, hasn't raised their prices in twenty years—and the price is listed on a drop-down menu on their website. Let freedom ring!

My Second Eye-Opening Moment

The second big positive moment in my career hit me after finding out about that piece of legislation that passed in June of 2019—and became available to any size business on January 1, 2020. This dramatic piece of legislation doesn't attack the costs of healthcare (Dave Chase and the Health Rosetta warriors are fighting that good fight) but allows employers to disconnect from the risk-management side of healthcare altogether.

This relatively unknown piece of legislation allows businesses the freedom to operate outside of the big Obamacare-employer-mandate penalties. This opens the door to the old-style cafeteria plans that used to be very popular in the 1980s and 1990s. Companies can once again give tax-free money to employees, allow them to buy and own their own health insurance, and customize it to fit the needs of them and their families. Using this new piece of legislation, the individual-coverage health-reimbursement arrangement (ICHRA), allows a company to offer something that was required under Obamacare (called minimum essential coverage or MEC) for companies with over fifty full-time equivalent employees. Obamacare required a company to provide this minimum essential coverage, or the company would have to pay a huge penalty of *$2,500.00 per employee per year* for simply not offering the kind of coverage the government deemed necessary. Now if you simply implement the ICHRA contract, this satisfies the minimum-essential-coverage requirement, and the company avoids this penalty altogether.

This represents a foundational change for healthcare management. This can be a little involved, but suffice it to say that many companies will enjoy this newfound freedom of not being attached to a health-insurance contract, and all that goes along with it. Strategies are already being adopted that have saved some companies as much as 40 to 60 percent on the costs of employee healthcare, depending on how much they were spending on their retail plans previous to this change. But most importantly, this model cuts out the disease completely—the disease of businesses being connected to health insurance—and the destruction involved in employers owning these contracts. You can now (for the first time in decades) allow your employees the choice *and the right* of ownership and control.

Imagine the freedom of no more health-insurance renewals for your business or your staff and the newfound freedom to control your budget each and every year. You just decide how much tax-free money to provide all of your employees at the end of each year—and that's it. No more complicated open-enrollment meetings, and no more worry about your insurance company raising your rates.

The decision on how much tax-free money to provide your employees each year should only take you about thirty to sixty minutes, rather than the four months of nonsense on your employer-owned retail plan design.

We'll see where all of this goes. We're only fifteen months into this newfound freedom as of the writing of this book. But most employers are completely unaware that their employees have many more positive choices in the marketplace than they do as employers. I think once employers start understanding that they can have a set budget for healthcare under this new strategy, they may start flocking to it like moths to a flame.

CHAPTER 6

FREEDOM, THE MODERN-DAY F-WORD

The word freedom today is avoided so much it's like profanity. Even the most successful people in the world don't talk about freedom—not Warren Buffett, not Jeff Bezos, not Bill Gates—nor many other successful entrepreneurs. They give away millions upon millions—and even billions of dollars—to different causes and organizations, but they rarely promote freedom while doing it.

Now, don't get me wrong, I'm not saying philanthropy is not an extremely important thing. But Mark Zuckerberg talked about giving away $45 billion in a 2000-word article saying how he was going to improve humanity in many different ways, and yet he never mentioned the word *freedom* once, despite freedom being the greatest improver of humanity's condition in history.

Just giving money away to people, by contrast, doesn't help them flourish.

Here are two obvious examples:

1. There are many desperately poor countries around the world. If someone like Bill Gates gave billions of dollars to one of these poor countries, and it was run by a

dictator that received that money and controlled it, the money would likely never get to the poor people who really needed it.

2. Here is a much more basic example. We all raise our children with the idea of helping them become responsible adults and be able to stand on their own two feet. Unless our children have severe disabilities or are unable to support themselves—who in their right mind would continue to give their thirty- to forty-year-old children $30,000 to $40,000 each year and expect them to become responsible adults? This would prevent them from having any incentive to work and earn money on their own. In other words, we would be blocking them from becoming responsible adults and realizing their own freedoms.

Why am I citing these examples?

Because giving people healthcare, through your benefits, creates a serious sense of dependency. If you are purchasing healthcare on behalf of your employees without involving them from the very beginning and giving them choices, you will likely never get any sense of true buy-in and *real appreciation* at all. When employees have a sense of ownership and control, it changes the dynamic completely. They feel empowered with their own sense of freedom and thus become more intimately involved with every element of their healthcare plans. Most employees have no idea what their employers have to deal with behind the scenes—but educating employees is an absolutely essential element to transforming a health plan. Most employers, if they took the time to really educate their employees, would find out that employees are hungry for more information and truly want to be involved in making their own healthcare plan better. This is true whether the employer owns the healthcare contract, or simply provides tax-free money to employees and allows them to customize their own healthcare. Employers tend to be very paternalistic or maternalistic. They rarely offer their employees the chance of feeling truly engaged in their healthcare decision process. They mostly say, "Here's what we provide for you." They try to put their best sales face on and say, "Isn't this great"? And still, the employees know that it really isn't that great at all.

The mountains of rules and regulations have turned healthcare into an increasingly complex and expensive industry, that isn't subjected to any free-market principles whatsoever.

This is also true for other industries. Take nuclear power as an example. Nuclear power produces energy density at a rate one million times greater than anything else ever created on earth. You can get as much energy from one uranium-filled golf ball as you can from filling all of Yankee Stadium to the rafters with coal. Yet, so many government rules and regulations stand in the way, that it takes fifteen to twenty years to get just one nuclear power plant built in this country. Bill Gates even started his own company called Terra Power; it powers nuclear plants using pre-viously-disposed-of nuclear-waste material. This significantly increases the safety levels of the nuclear energy source while producing the same energy density. Yet, the rules and regula-tions blocking this incredibly powerful energy source are stag-gering. Even Bill Gates, with all of his money and influence, has found it hard to make progress on the nuclear front. In a sense, it has made nuclear energy sufficiently illegal.

Healthcare has similarly been hamstrung by a seemingly in-surmountable stack of rules and regulations. In 2010, the federal government passed Obamacare—an enormous healthcare bill that dictated to the states, insurance companies, employers, and individuals a set of rules and penalties that has stifled innovation for a full decade.

The federal government dictated to the states. The states dictated to the insurance companies. Insurance companies dictated to businesses. Businesses had to dictate to their employees. And employees were left not knowing what just hit them! Even individuals outside of the workforce had to deal with an entirely different set of nonsensical rules and regulations. The government had stepped in and *literally made it illegal* not to own health insurance. Whether you agreed or disagreed about this part, I would hope we can all come together and conclude that this does not represent anything close to freedom.

The states have now set up something they call "insurance exchanges" for individuals who want to purchase health insurance on their own. These exchanges allow those people who don't have adequate funding from their employer-sponsored insurance to buy health insurance at reduced premium prices, depending on their household incomes. In fact, in 2021 they have just passed a law that states anyone buying their own individual or family insurance coverage (for the next two years) will not pay any more that 8.5% of their total income.

Confused? You're not alone.

The word freedom is looked upon as a different kind of animal in today's economic world. No one talks about it because there is a growing sentiment that top-down planning and government control lead to better results. *Nothing could be further from the truth!*

When I was in high school and college, freedom was discussed incessantly. It was so important to everyone in our circles that it was a source of pride, something we recognized and loved as individuals. Many bands played inspiring songs about freedom. Popular books about cherished freedoms circulated amongst friends. It was easy to see that America was a pretty special place when compared to communist Russia, China, and most other countries that controlled their citizens with top-down dictatorships, ruling from above.

As I write this today, people all around America believe that somehow our government knows what's best for us, rather than us being able to figure things out for ourselves. It is truly a difficult and sad time for America.

In the business community, the ability to act without forcible restraint by others is a very big deal. The more rules and regulations put on business owners that inhibit their production of goods and services, the less they can innovate and change marketplaces. When we are given absolute freedom to act without hindrance, problems get solved quickly. I'm not saying that laws aren't important. But too many laws create a stagnation of innovation and an overabundance of red tape. Today's doctors spend two hours tending to administrative tasks for every one hour spent with a patient.

The public is left with a system in which nobody knows what anything costs anymore. As an example, imagine going to your local clinic with a fracture and having to get an X-ray. Your insurance company might tell you that the X-ray typically costs $800, but you get a "network discount," so you'll only be charged $500. Then, when all is said and done, you get a statement from the clinic charging you $1,500 because you mistakenly went to an out-of-network clinic. You gulp before reading on and seeing something that says that your responsibility is $1,100. Then, after all of that, you find out that the cash price for the same X-ray for someone who doesn't have health insurance would have been only $150. What in the world is going on here?

Hence the name of this book.

Now, if free-market principles were in play, getting an X-ray would work the same way as choosing a restaurant. You would have the option of googling "X-rays for fractures" and sifting through the many different providers online. You would be able to compare quality-of-service and find pricing ahead of time. Furthermore, the pricing would be reasonable because, with more providers and less regulation, pricing would be competitive, as would the quality of your healthcare services. If you have a life-threatening situation today, like needing heart surgery, would you know who to go to for the best results? We can be faced with life-or-death decisions today—and not even know where to go to get the best help. What kind of system is that? It isn't a system that anyone in America should find acceptable.

The Invisible Hand

I'd like to digress for a moment and tell you about an inspirational moment in my life that changed my thinking forever, and launched me on this effort to explain to employers and employees what they can do about our health-insurance mess.

I was alone, watching a documentary called The Power of Choice: The Life and Ideas of Milton Friedman. Friedman was an influential economist who advocated for individual choice instead of top-down control. He believed that allowing the broader populations a "disparate say" in their personal choices prevented governments and larger organizations from dictating and distorting the prices of goods and services. In short, he was a warrior for the free-enterprise system, and had an undying respect for the common man.

In one part of this documentary, Alan Greenspan (the former Federal Reserve chairman) was describing Milton Friedman. He said, "There are very few people over the generations who have ideas that are sufficiently original to materially alter the direction of civilization. Milton is one of those very few people."

I sat and pondered this statement. This one man had original ideas *that literally altered the direction of civilization?!*

One man, with only his ideas, didn't just alter a city, state, or country, but actually altered our entire world's population? What made his ideas so powerful as to change the entire world? I realized that at the core of what he advocated was simply freedom. He advocated not just for political freedom—but specifically economic freedom as well. When economic and political freedom are secured, human flourishing naturally advances, making everyone's lives better. A rush went through my body like electricity running through my veins.

This is the key to the betterment of people all over the world: Freedom!

It's not talked about much in the news, but over one billion people have been lifted from extreme poverty over the last fifteen to twenty years. That is incredible when you stop to think about it. How did this happen? It was primarily due to countries like India and China allowing freer markets to exist within their own economies for the first time ever. If we want things to improve around the world, freedom needs to flourish.

Obviously, one person alone can't accomplish this kind of widespread freedom. People need many advocates in order to change any system for the better. Milton Friedman had many advocates to support his efforts, but most of his inspiration came from his own personal hero, Adam Smith, famous for coining the phrase "the invisible hand."

So, what is the invisible hand, and why is it so important to the subject of healthcare and health insurance?

Adam Smith developed the concept of the invisible hand in his book, The Theory of Moral Sentiment in 1759, and it is still extremely relevant today. The invisible hand is essentially a way of describing how, left free to pursue their separate interests, individuals achieve shared progress and prosperity. It suggests that too much regulation and government interference stifles innovative ideas and prevents mankind from flourishing. Free competition and choice ensure society's needs are reasonably met with competitive pricing and high-quality products and services. He later wrote the book The Wealth of Nations, which illustrated in great detail how the free-market system could work, and he changed the world of economics forever. He was able to show that allowing individuals the freedom to make their own decisions not only advanced human flourishing in an economic sense but, in turn, was an absolute moral imperative toward the betterment of mankind. The invisible hand became a shining example for countries around the world to emulate. Oddly enough, The Wealth of Nations was published on March 9 of the year 1776.

When it comes to healthcare, that invisible hand has been hog-tied. Or maybe it would be more representative to say that the very visible hand of Washington, DC, is reaching into the shallow pockets of employers and employees and redistributing their hard-earned dollars into the extremely deep pockets of insurance companies, healthcare providers, and many times, complicit brokerage firms.

Employers must understand that they don't need to be pigeonholed into insurance plans that cut into their employees' paychecks—sometimes deeper than even their employees' mortgage payments. Furthermore, employers need to know that other options exist beyond annual premium increases and mediocre health services. They should know that they can do much better for their employees—without taking a detrimental hit to their budgets each and every year.

Not Good Enough

Adam Smith and Milton Friedman both believed so strongly in the free-market system that a major part of their lives' work became showing others just how beneficial freedom is to human flourishing. But you don't need to be a world-renowned economist to realize exactly what a free-enterprise system does to products in the marketplace. We witness it every day with everything from hygiene products, to food and clothing, cell phones, computers, household goods—you name it. If a product is not heavily regulated, it will be subject to consumer choice and competition in our marketplace. When this happens, we see rising quality and falling prices.

Let's look at the evolution of cell phones as an example. In the 1970s, the first cellular telephone was released. It was the equivalent to a brick in both size and weight—and wasn't far off when considering functionality. You could make a call, but that's where it ended, and the battery lasted a mere twenty minutes. With no other competition on the market, Motorola was able to set the price point of this phone at nearly $4,000.

Now our phones have become our computers, cameras, organizers, and much more. Their batteries are capable of lasting for days, and the prices are astounding. Two-for-one phone deals are even common.

And it's not just our cell phones. Where free enterprise operates, we see this pattern of progress again, and again, and again.

But we don't see this in healthcare and health insurance. The American healthcare system got the shaft in the form of excessive rules and regulations coming from every angle imaginable.

I'm not saying freedom is completely absent from the healthcare industry. It can be found, but currently, it is hidden from plain sight.

The good news is that, for the first time in a very long time, free-market principles are being brought to the table in the healthcare and health insurance space. They are dramatically and fiercely fighting for the consumer and business owners around this country in order to reduce the cost of health insurance and clean up our healthcare mess. This movement is spreading like wildfire and is bringing dynamic solutions. The true warriors in this space have an attitude that screams the words, "It's never *EVER* good enough" every day of their lives. They see the breakthroughs that I have seen, and they'll never quit innovating until they make things just a little better each and every day.

So, what are these alternatives to traditional healthcare and employer-owned health-insurance contracts? More are entering the market every year, but we'll start with a short-list of some of the most attractive alternatives within the marketplace today: Coalition plans, PEOs, HRAs, and Custom health plans.

Coalition Plans

Coalition plans are a subset of custom health plans but are worth mentioning in a separate category of their own. These plans enable employers to pay lower rates due to a dramatic method of risk reduction. When it comes to health-insurance costs, larger companies are generally given lower insurance rates because the risk is distributed over a much larger population. Because smaller businesses do not have these same large numbers, they needed to find other ways to reduce that risk. Now, owners of small to midsize companies can band together with other companies around the nation to get the much larger numbers required to minimize their risk.

Coalition plans are essentially a collaborative network of like-minded employers managed by an organization that acts in the best interest of all parties. This allows them to provide optimal value for all parties involved.

Hundreds of these coalition plans are popping up all over the country. We implemented a coalition plan for a company of only sixty-six employees at the beginning of 2019. It reduced their premiums by 33 percent, and all of the healthcare benefits for the employees remained exactly the same. Their total cost went from $684,000 to $458,000 in ninety days.

In this particular coalition plan, employees were able to get free-market pricing and get directed to the highest-quality, best-priced medical care through a uniquely formed concierge service. These concierge services provide smartphone technologies that connect employees to the best prices for different healthcare procedures, prescription drugs, X-rays, MRIs, and much more. Many of these newly formed concierge companies are now demanding health outcomes from their contracted healthcare providers. This is one of those categories of this business that is at the early stages of development, but I say, *it's about time!*

Most coalition plans even pay dividends back to employers at the end of each year due to the overall savings of the coalition portfolio. Based on the performance of the overall coalition, this sixty-six-person company is positioned to receive an additional $50,000 to $100,000 at the end of the year.

The caveat of these coalition plans is that not all companies are eligible to join. Often a series of stipulations may need to be met first before allowing a company to participate. Knowledgeable healthcare consultants can help navigate the individual coalition guidelines, and position companies to have everything in place prior to applying for a coalition.

Professional-Employer Organization (PEO)

Professional-employer organizations are an effective way for businesses to outsource their employee benefits, and leave the administration of these benefits in the hands of someone more qualified. PEOs are made up of a collective group of businesses that join together to offer employee benefits to their employees. PEOs cater primarily to small and midsize businesses, which are able to outsource an array of services to help them to save both time and money—as the PEOs operate on a much larger scale than any single small or midsize business.

PEOs are not only focused on healthcare and health insurance. PEOs provide a suite of benefits from human resources, payroll services, workers compensation, regulatory and compliance assistance, 401(k)s, and much more. Offering benefits through a PEO will give your employees access to a Fortune 500 choice of products and services and leave the administrative burden in their hands. PEOs are able to get the same lower-risk pricing of larger companies because they actually pool together all of the employers under the PEO umbrella.

Several variations of PEOs exist, but through each of these co-employment models, one thing is true: better rates are usually obtained, and benefits packages are expanded dramatically. The important thing to understand is your co-employment contract with your PEO. You see, the way they can legally offer a PEO is by forming a separate company (with benefits) and allowing your company to hitch your wagon to theirs. Make sure you take the time to understand everything about this co-employment contract, as well as how much your per employee costs are for hitching your wagon to this model. This model allows small to midsize businesses to attract and retain a much more skilled workforce by offering a wide variety of benefits that can compete with much larger companies in the marketplace. Furthermore, because the PEO firm is handling all of the administrative burdens, these businesses are more fully able to focus on their own business at hand.

The truly great PEOs in the marketplace now allow employers to carve out their health plans, and customize them to fit their own particular philosophies and needs. Sometimes, a PEO may be able to provide so much savings on just an employer's carve-out health plan, that it can literally pay for the cost of the entire PEO-monthly-service fee.

Brokerage firms do not sell PEOs, so they will definitely not tell you about this solution—they'd lose your business!

HRAs

HRA stands for health-reimbursement arrangement. An HRA resides inside the new cafeteria-plan designs I talk about in this book. It is an account that is created on behalf of the employee by the employer. Funds are deposited into this account and may be used by the employee for health-insurance premiums. The same HRA can also be used to pay out-of-pocket medical expenses, such as co-pays and deductibles, all tax-free. With HRAs, the employee is given a monthly allowance to spend as they wish. HRAs are not the same as your traditional employer-provided health-insurance plans, they are simply reimbursement models that enable employees to choose healthcare options that are right for them and their families, and pay for that coverage with pre-tax money.

Many businesses that either can't afford to pay for a fully insured retail-health plan, or don't want their business to be "connected to a health-insurance contract," choose to offer HRAs instead. This provides employees a way to customize their own individually owned plans. Let's face it, you have employees that are young and old, singles and families, healthy and unhealthy. Allowing them to choose what's right for them is better than saying, "Here's our health-insurance plan, hope it fits you!"

The big advantage here is that the employees actually *own* the healthcare contract, not the employer. The employer provides the funds in a cafeteria-type fashion. Using this method detaches the employer from any claims that are incurred on behalf of their individual employees.

This is a stark departure from how companies have provided health benefits in the past. These cafeteria plans were extremely popular for small to midsize businesses back in the '80s and '90s when rules and regulations weren't getting in the way of healthcare. Now that the penalties have been sufficiently eliminated for both businesses and individuals, this may prove to be a common-sense solution for any size business in the coming years. There are different styles of HRAs that are brand new in 2020. Finding the right one for your company is relatively easy. Third-party administrators (TPAs) in the HRA space allow your HR Director to do all of the reimbursements at the push of a button through your already-existing payroll accounts. Most of these TPAs can assist you in navigating which HRA will be the proper choice for you. There's the qualified-small-employer health-reimbursement arrangement (QSEHRA), the excepted-benefit health-reimbursement arrangement (EBHRA), or the brand-new individual-coverage health-reimbursement arrangement (ICHRA). I know that's a mouthful, but don't get too caught up in the acronym-world of healthcare at this point. I'm just pointing out that there are choices available now that were not available before—choices that can often dramatically reduce the cost of business healthcare. There is even a new TPA in the marketplace that will deliver all of the employee's premiums directly to the insurance companies on behalf of your employees. It looks and feels just like an employer-owned group plan. The company helps set the coverage up on behalf of each employee, pays all the premiums, and provides the same payroll deductions for employees just like a group plan works today. The biggest difference this model provides, is that the employer is in complete control of their budget going forward.

In case you didn't understand that last sentence let me say it again. With the HRA, *the employer is in complete control of their healthcare budget going forward.*

Ok, now I can move on.

Custom Health Plans

Custom health plans are ones in which the employer, rather than the insurance provider, assumes the associated risk of providing healthcare. Essentially, the employer sets up an account that is used to pay for their employees' healthcare claims. These self-funded plans can work similarly to a fully insured retail plan, with the employer and the employee contributing to the insurance plan's premiums. They differ, however, in that healthcare funds (within the self-insured plan) that are unused at the end of the year can be retained by the employer to utilize as they see fit.

Remember that, statistically, an employer will only use the full amount of their reserves in two out of every five years, which means that they will retain those unused reserves for the other three years. These reserves can be used as the employer sees fit—to give raises, increase other benefits, or even help a business get through a difficult year in business. Another reason why employers often choose to use a custom health plan is that they are not subject to federal regulations and state premium taxes, which allows them to save additional money. Custom health plans are revolutionizing the prices of our healthcare systems, because employers have more control and freedom over how to spend their healthcare dollars. The number, size, and frequency of your employees' healthcare claims are being measured and controlled because it is now *your money being spent*, not the insurance company's. Hospitals, out-patient-surgery centers, pharmacy benefit managers, and even primary-care physicians are being put in a position of competing for your healthcare business in the new digital healthcare world. Using a custom health-plan design can be beneficial in many ways. One of the truly nice things about switching to a custom design is that your HR team can use the same systems they currently use for enrollments and every other administrative system. It stays the same because you (the employer) still own the contract.

These four alternatives (listed above) to fully-insured traditional retail health plans are among the least-known alternatives within the marketplace, but they aren't the only ones. As free-market principles are being reintroduced to the marketplace, so is an array of new and improved innovative solutions.

The difficult part is finding out about these alternative solutions. Your current broker can't provide all of these solutions through their brokerage firm. You can't expect your broker to offer you every alternative solution that exists in the marketplace. Just mentioning any of the aforementioned solutions could not only significantly reduce a broker's revenue streams, but could even result in them losing your business.

Would you talk about these alternatives if you were a broker?

Now let's look at the main reasons behind today's outrageous health-insurance prices.

CHAPTER 7

UNLIMITED CREDIT CARDS — ZERO INTEREST AND NO REPAYMENT REQUIRED

Warning: this might wrinkle your brain!

As I mentioned before, employers are paying right around $15,000 per employee per year for health insurance. This means that a company with as few as twenty employees is paying close to $300,000 a year for health coverage. And companies with just one hundred employees can, in many cases, face an annual budget of $1,500,000.

Keep in mind that those numbers are averages. Midsized businesses (companies of 50–1000 employees) are often paying much more than that for their traditional retail plans. A company of just 80 employees could have just a few bad claims that may collectively cost $2 million. If they only paid $1 million in premiums in the year those high claims happen, the insurance company will want to recover that loss in the subsequent year. Come renewal time, they would likely want to charge the company 30 to 40 percent more in premiums if they want to keep their coverage.

The financial impact of healthcare costs hits businesses harder and harder every year. That same company of twenty employees might have to fork over an additional $40,000 to $60,000 at the end of the year, just to keep their exact same level of coverage. That is just sick and wrong!

Allow me to provide some perspective as to why this whole thing has gotten so out of hand.

Imagine you signed up for a new credit card. Now, this credit card isn't just any credit card—it's special. With this credit card, you pay a monthly fee and can use it as much as you want without capping out at a designated spending limit. That's right: this particular credit card will never be maxed-out, so you'll never have the embarrassment of being declined at checkout. And it gets better. Once you have charged a certain amount (let's say $4,000) each year, you are allowed to spend literally as much as you want for the rest of the year *for free*. You do have to pay back the $4000, but after that, the sky's the limit. You may charge $10,000, $100,000, or even $1,000,000, and you only have to pay back the $4000.

If you're smart, you're going to put everything on that one credit card and will never use any of your other cards again, right? After all, once you have spent $4000, everything is absolutely free. You aren't even going to search for the best deals on your purchases past $4000. You aren't going to inquire as to why prices are what they are on those purchases, and you certainly aren't going to hold back on how much you spend.

Now imagine you were selling a product or service and you found out a customer is paying you with one of these special credit cards. Would you charge him the same price you charge everyone else? If he doesn't care about the price of your offerings, are you going to make them as affordable as possible—or as expensive as possible?

Well, this is how the health insurance industry operates today. That unlimited-expense credit card is your employee's health-insurance cards. You and your employees pay the premiums every month, and should you have any medical expenses, your employees pay your first $4000 (or whatever the out-of-pocket maximum is on your employer's insurance plan), and that's it. Once they reach their out-of-pocket maximums, they won't have to pay a dime for healthcare services, prescription drugs, and the like for the rest of that year.

It really doesn't matter how many times you go to the doctor; what procedures are being done, or whether it fixes your problem or not. You have an unlimited amount of money to use each and every year. No interest accrues on this money, and you never have to pay it back—ever!

See what I mean—unlimited credit card, no interest, and no repayment.

Here are some questions for you to ponder at this point:

- Do you know which of your employees are using this "unlimited healthcare" strategy to their advantage? And would you blame them for doing this?
- Are you aware that just a few high healthcare spenders can affect all of your other healthy employees with much higher premiums at your year-end renewal time?
- Have you ever wondered why the collective healthcare costs of your entire employee population are all lumped together for insurance pricing considerations?

- Have you ever considered allowing your employees to own their own health insurance coverage so that one employee's claims can never *ever* impact another employee?

Here's why this problem is such a major issue for the people within the healthcare industry as well as the patients:

When a person can spend endless amounts of money to fix something, those doing the "fixing" begin to charge more, and the quality of the "fixing" begins to suffer. There is no real incentive to fix your medical problems. If they don't actually fix your problem, they don't even get any kind of penalties. Now, I'm not saying doctors and nurses don't want to fix your problems. But, do they list their healthcare results on their websites, so that you know how likely it is that your knee replacement will be successful? Do you know what their rates of infections are at that healthcare facility or hospital? When you go into these places, you aren't even told the prices to undergo their tests and procedures. But, if you have hit your limit of $4,000 already, do you really care? You should, but most people don't. And if your medical problem didn't get fixed, at least you didn't have to pay. See how weird this is?

Try asking your doctor what it costs for a particular procedure when you go in for a visit. Next time you need an X-ray, ask them the price of that X-ray. Chances are, the person taking your insurance card at the clinic doesn't even know and will likely respond, "You will have to speak with your insurance company about that." Does any of this sound just plain wrong to you at all?

Here's the thing. This isn't free money at all. Someone is paying for this.

"Nobody spends other people's money as carefully as they spend their own."
— Milton Friedman, economist

So, whose money is being spent? Ultimately the employers and their employees are paying these bills in the form of ever-increasing premiums. The health insurers offering you that "special credit card" don't want to go broke. They want to make money. So, once the end of the year rolls around, they are going to raise the premiums drastically for the same coverage, and both the employers and the employees will take the hit. Your "free" healthcare spending this year is going to be paid for in more expensive health insurance premiums the very next year. And the more you spend on your healthcare, the more the insurance companies make. Check their share prices over the last decade if you don't believe me!

The truth is, no checks and balances exist at all within this system—not with the quality of care, the cost of care, or eventually your ever-increasing health-insurance rates. This is how your fully insured retail-health-insurance plan is set up to work. It's set up to work for the benefit of the insurance companies, pharmacy companies, and hospitals, not employers or employees.

This is an enormous problem. America is spending trillions of dollars each and every year behind this unlimited-credit-card system.

Our Medicare credit-card system is even worse. These dollars are backed by the American taxpayers. Your trusted politicians are controlling this money. Ever looked behind the curtain to see if our safe-and-sound Medicare system is running a surplus?

Oh, don't even go there with me.

CHAPTER 8

LITTLE-KNOWN TRUTHS

B y now, you've probably already thought to yourself, "But wait, how did the health insurance situation ever get to be this bad?"

- Didn't someone recognize that there was a major problem building up decades ago?
- Weren't our politicians aware that this was happening?
- Weren't the chambers of commerce organizations around the country alerted to this issue?
- Isn't someone at some higher-level of knowledge trying to do something to right the ship?

Problems like this can't be solved by what I call top-down planning. The truth of the matter is that *top-down planning is what has caused this problem in the first place.* We can lay most all of this mess at the feet of our beloved politicians, both left and right.

Let me illustrate once more. Our politicians pass laws at the federal level. The state's politicians pass laws regulating all of their insurance companies. The insurance companies (who must adhere to the laws and guidelines from the federal and state governments) provide their own set of rules to employers.

Employers then buy their own healthcare contracts, and make most of the decisions on behalf of their employees. See the top-down scenario? The employees were never even in the equation during the decision-making. If they were left alone to decide for themselves, this whole mess would likely never have occurred.

Let me give you a brief history lesson, touching on the primary events that got us to where we are today.

A. Wage & Price Controls

In 1942, economy-wide wage and price controls were established at below free-market prices as a response to inflation, and to help keep costs lower during wartime. This decision was deemed necessary (in many ways) to help in the war effort to defeat the Nazis and the Japanese during WWII. But the unintended result was that businesses weren't able to compete for quality workers based on starting pay or willingness to provide pay raises. So, they began offering healthcare to employees as a way to offer greater benefits without providing more pay.

This is really where business-owned health plans began. Businesses would cover healthcare costs as a means of attracting and retaining top employees. Eventually, this became so popular that the government introduced "temporary" legislation for companies to offer healthcare tax-free. Over seventy-five years later, this "temporary" legislation still stands.

At the time this was first implemented, the employer would cover the premium (fully tax-deductible for them) with either a zero deductible or a very small deductible for each employee. Employees would have almost 100 percent of their health insurance and their healthcare costs covered by their employer. Who wouldn't love that!?

It was great for the employees, but there was one major problem: the scenario of the unlimited credit card with no repayment that we discussed in the previous chapter had begun. Also, businesses were now treated as owning their own "mini-insurance company" within their own business. The business-owned healthcare plans had to manage the risk within their own employee populations. Back then, health-insurance companies were also able to assess the risk for their employer-owned health-insurance plans. For decades, these insurance companies would have employees fill out health-history applications as part of the enrollment process. This way, the insurance companies could calculate their risk by seeing the overall health of the collective employees. Eventually, state laws were passed dictating to the health-insurance companies that all employer-owned healthcare was mandated to have a "no pre-existing condition" requirement within their contracts. This meant that if an employer hired a person with diabetes that regularly racked up $150,000 to $200,000 in yearly claims, the employer had to charge that employee the same rate as their healthy employees. Risk management had begun to go away for the health-insurance companies. The dirty little secret was that all insurance companies had a loop-hole to deal with the government's rules. Raise insurance rates systematically, year-by-year, until premium payments are higher than car payments, and many times higher than mortgage payments for American families.

B. The Affordable Care Act

The federal government passed the Patient Protection Affordable Care Act (PPACA), i.e., Obamacare, in 2010 and rolled it out fully by 2014. This law stated that no health insurance company (not employer-owned or individually-owned) in the

United States could ask any medical questions when you bought a standard health-insurance plan. The pre-existing conditions clause now states that no health insurance company *in the nation* can ask anyone about their history of obesity, cancer, diabetes, heart disease, strokes, or anything else related to your health.

While many people applauded our government, thinking it was the best decision for our public as a whole, those within the health-insurance community were straight-up giddy about this national healthcare law. They knew exactly what was about to go down, and many insurance companies happened to be at the table agreeing that the legislation should be signed and passed. That should have been a *huge red flag* for all of us!

What these companies understood (that the general population did not) was that once they were unable to manage the overall risk of the population, they were free to raise premiums across the board. How much did they raise everybody's premiums? This was different in each state, but the amount was substantial, and has typically averaged about 6 to 8 percent year-after-year. Some individual states raised their individual health insurance rates more than 100 percent in a single year. Arizona ended up having the highest rate increase when between 2016 and 2017, they raised their individual health insurance rates 145 percent.

It should also be noted (once again) that share prices of insurance companies have seen a massive uptick since the bill was passed in 2010. While most Americans are struggling to obtain affordable coverage and spending more and more each year, insurance companies themselves are profiting greatly. All of this happened because of one piece of extreme federal government regulation—the Affordable Care Act. That's why many today call it the Unaffordable Care Act.

Were there some good things that came about because of the Obamacare bill? Most definitely. In the last chapter of this book, I will be talking at length about these positive aspects. In fact, I will be pointing out how you can use these positive elements, within your employer-healthcare plan, to ensure that some employees' health-insurance rates never increase in the future. I know this also sounds too-good to be true. But you haven't heard (as the old-time radio announcer Paul Harvey used to say) the rest of the story. Never heard of Paul Harvey? Google it.

C. Penalties and Disincentives

There have been an array of rules and regulations with associated penalties and unintended consequences that came with the Affordable Care Act, leading to a further deterioration of our free-market system.

The employer mandate, established by the Affordable Care Act, stated that every employer with over fifty full-time-equivalent employees (FTEs) would get charged $2000 per employee each year if they chose to cancel their employer-owned group health-insurance plan. This charge had gone up to $2500 per employee per year as of 2020. By the way, the term "full-time equivalent" was not even a term until the Obamacare law was put into effect.

This mandate meant that if any employer in America had over fifty full-time equivalent employees, and offered a different type of healthcare plan than what the federal government said was proper, they would be fined that $2500 per employee per year penalty.

People on the individual health-insurance market were also charged a fine if they did not buy health-insurance coverage for themselves or their families. A stiff penalty was assessed by the IRS for individuals or families who didn't buy the type of coverage the government thought they should buy.

The government also announced (in 2013) that they would charge employers an additional amount of **$100 per employee per day** for reimbursing employees for individual health insurance instead of offering employer-owned retail health plans. Once certified public accountants (CPAs) discovered this, they advised employers across America to play ball with the government rules or else! Back then, the only reasonable option for a small to midsize company was to continue with the destructive employer-owned retail group health plans or pay the piper. They literally had no other reasonable options. *It was the exact opposite of freedom.* Fortunately, they overturned this unreasonable $100 per employee per day penalty in June of 2015, but the coerciveness was obvious. Top-down planning seemed like it was here to stay!

Let's look at an analogous scenario, using a car as an example:

Imagine gas prices went up to $6/gallon next year, then up to $10/gallon the following year, $15/gallon the year after that, $25, $40, and so on. Eventually, gas prices would be so out of control that folks would be looking for other alternatives to their gas-powered vehicles.

Now imagine that the government stepped in and told everybody in the country that they *had to buy gas* for their cars or they would be penalized. In other words, it would become illegal to own any other type of transportation beyond a gasoline-powered car. If you owned an electric car to fight against these policies, they would charge you so much in penalties that you could lose your car. This sounds ridiculous, right? But, that's essentially the exact same scenario that had been happening with healthcare. With previous insurance hikes of almost 400 percent over the last twenty years, it simply added insult to injury.

The good news: as of 2020, most of these rules and penalties associated with the Affordable Care Act have now been wiped out. New incentives have been implemented advancing free-market forces, and this Bobby Thompson "shot heard around the world" is changing the game of healthcare. But this shot is not nearly loud enough for me. My ERISA attorney firm is constantly exploring every legal avenue for employers big and small to utilize these new concepts. We are looking to put the incentives (and the decisions) back into the hands of the employers and their employees, not politicians and insurance companies.

You can now own a contract that allows you to put untaxed money into your own business account and control exactly how your money is to be spent on your employees' healthcare each and every month. If at the end of the year, your claims don't exceed the funds in your account, your company keeps that money. As I previously mentioned, employers will typically experience one to two bad claim years out of every five. This is a pretty strong incentive for business owners to retain some of this operating expense and to redirect some of that money back to their bottom line. This is *not* how your traditional employer retail healthcare plan works. But many employers are still operating under this broken "retail-plan" system.

You can also set aside tax-free money and allow your employees to choose their own levels of coverage through an individual health plan. In some states, including my own state of Minnesota, individual rates are much lower than company-owned group plans. This is not true for every state in the union, so you will have to do your own due diligence, but this represents a dramatic departure allowing individual contract ownership rather than corporate ownership.

This could provide a clear future path for companies that never wanted to be in the business of healthcare in the first place—and is a pretty strong incentive to break free from the old 1942 design, and bring their business into the twenty-first century.

As a nation, we have the ability to dig ourselves out of this highly regulated healthcare mess. We just need to have access to this information and be willing to move forward with some of these seemingly "too-good-to-be-true" alternatives!

D. Private Property Rights

Employer's Rights

I never really thought too deeply about how property rights would apply to health insurance for businesses until about a decade ago.

But first I need to take you back in time for a moment.

When the pilgrims came to this country they tried to live in a collective way. Meaning, they didn't own the land that they lived on individually, but they owned it collectively as a group. What this meant (over time) was that no one really took care of their own individual plot of land, because they didn't truly own the property. No one individual had private property rights. Only when they tried a new system, in which everyone owned their own plot of land, did they truly start to take care of their property in every way. They realized that when they aligned the incentives properly, the pilgrims began to take pride in what they owned.

Years ago one of my employer groups wanted to shop for different coverage, but we found out (because of bad claims) no other group insurance company wanted to cover them. They were simply too high of a risk. I had no other choice but to see what the options looked like on the individual health insurance marketplace. It turned out that the premiums were almost 40 percent less for individual insurance plans here in Minnesota back then. I converted their group plan to individual coverage. This was back when the individual insurance carriers could ask medical questions. Most people don't know this, but if you got declined for individual insurance back then, the states had fallback options to ensure anyone that got rejected was covered by a state plan. Almost every state in the union had this fallback option.

This took a lot of work transitioning this group and allowing every employee to choose the coverage that was right for them. We also had to coordinate with an administrator that would pay all of the premiums to the insurance providers on behalf of the employees. But the conversion allowed the employees to make their own choices, and empowered them to customize the coverage to what they wanted, not what their employer thought was best.

There are only two basic ways to offer healthcare to employees. The employer can own the health insurance/healthcare contract, or they can allow their employees to own their own contracts, and the employer can provide them dollars to help pay for that coverage.

If you are a company that still wants to own your own healthcare contract, you are hamstringing yourself in a number of different ways. You are not only paying higher premium prices, but you are playing the role of "risk manager" for no apparent reason.

Let me provide you with a simple illustration:

Any employee that works for you (past the age of 65) has the right to continue healthcare coverage with your company under the group insurance contract owned by your firm.

If I was an individual in the marketplace trying to buy health insurance, I would be forced to take Medicare coverage after age 65. The reason for this is simply because there is no health insurance in the individual marketplace that is even offered after the age of 65. Now this may be good or bad depending on your perception. But if I was your employee, I would love to stay on your employer-owned coverage, especially since you likely pay most of the cost of my premiums. Now, as an employer, you are paying for an employee to be on your plan that has a very high probability that they will have high claims after the age of 65. And when claims come in at ages 65 and above, the likelihood that these claims will be higher-priced claims goes up significantly!

If you are trying to be responsible in your "risk manager role", why would you put your company in a position to pay these high claims when you know higher claims equal higher premiums? This is just the tip of the iceberg relating to the complications of employers owning a healthcare contract.

Many large employers will still choose to own their own healthcare contract though for the simple reason of *ease of administration*. Yet, most employers today don't understand that they have the ability to take control of how their claims are being paid on behalf of their employees. Since the employer owns the contract, they have every right to use whatever means possible (legally) to control the claim costs within their organization.

Control the claims and you can control the premiums that you are being charged to hold that contract. Make sense?

I am not here to tell you that this is an easy task. But I am telling you that you have the right to control *every element of the health care contract* for your employees. Most employers do not even understand that this is even possible. And would it be a surprise to anyone that the big insurance and big pharmacy companies don't want you to know that this is possible?

If you choose to still own your healthcare contract (as an employer), utilize your constitutional rights as a private property owner and take control of your plan. When you take on the role of risk manager, allowing a "mini-insurance company" to be run inside of your company, you must protect your private property rights with a ruthless fervor like none other. You are putting the healthcare rights of your employees in your own hands. You better take this seriously!

Employee's Rights

If you are going to work for a company (and use their insurance coverage) you are essentially renting the health insurance from your employer. As an employee, you are literally disconnected from the total cost, how the coverage is designed, and any of the details related to your employer's contract. In fact, if you leave the company, you are only able to take the coverage with you under Cobra rules and regulations for about 18 months. Cobra regulations would have never been written if the government hadn't passed a big tax law back in 1942, allowing employers to fully deduct the healthcare and health insurance costs.

Alternatively, if you (the employee) owned the healthcare contract, that insurance coverage would be portable and you could take it with you no matter where you worked. I'm sorry, but doesn't this make good common sense to think health insurance should have always been this way?

How would it make you feel if your employer offered all of the employee's car insurance, then later you find out that a fellow employee got in two accidents last year, got a DUI, and made everyone's premiums go up by 30 percent? Wouldn't you question your employer's judgement on putting a policy like this in force in the first place?

I have wondered this for a long time now. Is it just me that feels this way?

E. Businesses Controlling Healthcare Costs, Not Insurance Companies
The retail-plan price model is quickly being replaced by different delivery methods within the healthcare industry. Why? It's actually quite simple.

Here's the *retail plan* model:

You give the insurance company all of your money. And then you . . .

- Let them price it,
- Let them deliver it,
- Let them renew it,
- Let them control it, and
- Let you pay for it!

As opposed to the *Custom plan* models:
Where . . .

- You price it,
- You deliver it,
- You renew it,
- You control it, and
- You reap the savings!

Employers all across America are waking up to the fact that they possess a lot more freedom than they ever thought they had in the area of healthcare. Since they are the ones providing most of the money to fund healthcare for employees in the first place, they are free to spend these dollars however they choose. Not only are they recognizing the fundamental differences in how they provide for their employees, but they are also recognizing that there is power in numbers.

Large employers can now receive a detailed analysis of the main cost-drivers within their healthcare plans. Hospital cost details, out-patient surgery breakdowns, prescription drug pricing, and even primary-care costs can be analyzed and repriced like never before. Direct contracts with hospitals and bundled-priced healthcare providers are bringing costs down by 20 to 40 percent. Prescription drugs are being re-sourced directly from the manufacturers, providing immediate cost reductions of as much as 40 to 70 percent.

Small to midsize employers are using cash prices within the exploding health-share industry to reprice their employees' costs for coverage. Since most hospitals have systems already set up for accepting cash-paying patients, it takes them no time at all to switch to a different technology resource and provide their patients with 40 to 60 percent price-reduction quotes within minutes.

Now, you may be saying to yourself, "I'm not going to be able to dictate to a hospital what they are going to charge me for things like quadruple bypass heart surgeries or liver transplants or cancer treatments." I'm here to tell you that it's being done all over the country to tremendous success.

Let's jump into some of the more creative ways that healthcare prices are being controlled across America.

CHAPTER 9

THE PRICE YOU PAY

Why Can't We Pay Cash?

This is a true-life story of something that happened to me and my wife on Christmas Eve night in 2018. My wife had been feeling awful most of the day, and by 11:00 p.m., she had complained about a severe soreness in her left arm. I rushed her to the emergency room at a hospital about fifteen minutes away. She received a number of tests and treatments and was fortunately found to have an infection and was going to be okay. She was released around 3:00 a.m. on Christmas morning. Oddly enough, they never asked either one of us for our insurance information. We had spent an exhausting four hours in an emergency room, but we were very grateful after all was said and done. We had coverage, but our coverage was through a health-sharing program and not a "health-insurance" plan. Many of these types of programs exist around the country, but we were covered under one that provided a "gold plan design," which provided each of us generous coverage for any medical occurrence. We were individually responsible for the first $500, and then they would pay the rest of the expenses with the other health-sharing members around the country.

Both in our very early sixties, my wife and I paid $344 a month in premiums for the two of us combined for this coverage. We switched to this coverage on August 21, 2018, when we found out that our high-deductible retail group plan (with a $4,000 deductible for each of us before the insurance paid anything) was going to be raised to $1,800 a month for the two of us.

Fast forward to about six weeks after the emergency room visit when we received our bill from the hospital. The total was $6,750 for everything done during her four-hour stay. This didn't surprise me at all, but what happened next astounded me. I called the billing department at the hospital to inquire about my bill. The first thing she asked me was, "What kind of insurance plan are you covered through?" I informed her that we didn't have health insurance and that we were cash-paying customers under a health-sharing plan. To my surprise, she responded, "Oh, okay, let me get to my other system here." She then simply plugged my billing into their "cash-payer" system, and ten minutes later, she told me she would be sending out a revised billing.

I asked how much that new revised billing would be, and after a long pause, she said:

Your revised bill comes to a total of $3,125.00.

So, in literally ten minutes, my bill was cut down by 53 percent. How was that possible?

As it turns out, there's almost always a reduction of 40 to 70 percent by providers when they find out you don't have traditional insurance coverage. When you pay *real cash money,* prices are more transparent and significantly lower. Now, I'm sure the $3,125 charge included a profit for the hospital, but we were fine with that. In fact, if they hadn't profited from treating my wife, I would have been upset! We paid our $500, and the health-sharing program paid the rest of our bill, which was shared by the 400,000 other members within our plan across the country.

I'm not telling you this story to have you run out and immediately join a health-sharing program or to tell you to go without insurance. I'm telling you this story to help you understand that the "price systems" out there are different depending on what type of coverage you have.

These different price systems are beginning to revolutionize how healthcare is being paid for and provided around the country. Just a couple of years ago, these health-sharing programs were just available through the individual marketplace. Now they are being offered to employers all around America. There are eight to ten different health-sharing organizations now, and some have been operating successfully for over forty years. Did you know that? Neither did I.

As consultants, we have our ways of finding out exactly what different facilities charge for different procedures. Most of our clients operate under custom self-insured plan designs, and the employers pay their claims themselves out of earnings rather than going through a retail-health-insurance-company price system. In other words, they are all analogous to cash-payers in some way, shape, and form.

Let's look at how this pricing game works. We'll use a knee replacement again as our example.

I know of many different places within my own state of Minnesota that perform these full knee replacements. They can vary in cost from about $26,000 to almost $90,000. It usually depends on which facility you see and which insurance company you use. These prices involve insurance carrier networks and are priced to include those "supposedly great" PPO discounts within each of these networks. Again, nothing prevents one facility from charging an insurance company $90,000 and another from charging $130,000. Both of the facilities would provide a network discount of some kind (usually 30 to 40 percent) and end up with a discount price between $54,000 and $85,000 for the full knee-replacement cost. The person getting their knee replaced would receive an explanation of benefits (EOB) in the mail spelling out all of these charges and discounts in their statement. But what do you look at when that statement comes in the mail? Immediately your eyes go to the bottom of the statement that says, "What You Owe," right? You may have to pay your $4,000 maximum, or if you've already incurred $4,000 in previous medical costs for the year, you may have already hit the max on your employer's insurance coverage.

When you see that "What You Owe" section saying $0.00, like most people, you probably breathe a big sigh of relief and just throw that EOB in the garbage. If you can relate to this story, you are not alone.

As one of my business owners asked, "You mean to tell me that a facility can charge $130,000 to eventually have the insurance company pay them $90,000—and nobody questions this behavior? What kind of a messed-up system is this?"

I told him this is called the American employer-healthcare system.

Price Interruptions

It's easy to understand how people tend to take advantage of a third-party-payor system. It's not only in health insurance that people use this to their advantage. Lawyers do it all the time. As soon as they know that a person has an insurance policy that will likely payout due to an accident or injury, they are quick to jump in and attach their fees to the winnings in a lawsuit. Car insurance, malpractice insurance, or any other type of insurance can be susceptible to interrupting the free-market price system.

Each state government is mandated by the federal government to manage and regulate the health-insurance companies operating within the state. After the ACA disrupted the states and insurance companies with their rules and regulations, it left some states and counties with only one health insurance-company choice. Imagine wanting to buy health insurance and being told you only have one company to choose from for yourself and your family?

So much for the good intentions of our politicians!

Ever wonder why we can buy car insurance anywhere in the USA, but you can only buy your health insurance coverage within your own state? Don't you think one of the mighty (and very profitable) insurance companies might be able to figure out a way to sell you a contract from Indiana even if you lived in Arkansas? I'll bet they could—and would even make sure that they made a healthy profit on that insurance-contract sale. What would that do for the basic economic principles of choice and competition? Imagine if 1,500 insurance companies were competing for your business rather than the handful that are within your home state. Do you think the prices might be different?

The state dictates its own set of rules and regulations to each insurance company that they must strictly abide by or face serious consequences. In fact, each insurance company must file their premium prices within each state to get "approval" before they file the "official rates" to sell to the general public. How messed up is that?

The health-insurance companies then dictate to employers their own set of guidelines. Minimum premium contributions need to be followed as well as participation rules and guidelines. Employers then are required to pass down their own sets of requirements to their employees. In my state, under the "retail-plan guidelines," if the employer doesn't pay at least 50 percent of the employee's premiums and if 50 percent of the employees don't participate in the plan, you can't even buy the insurance for your employees. Who made these rules? The state regulators and the insurance companies, that's who!

And if you didn't like it, you couldn't do a thing about it, until now. Minimum contribution rules and participation guidelines only apply if employers own the health insurance contract. By breaking free from ownership employers set their own standards. You can now decide how much money to provide your employees, and allow them to purchase what they want. It's your rules now, not the government's or the insurance company's rules.

Trying to keep up with all of the rules of healthcare is exhausting. What are the rules and guidelines I need to follow on HSAs, Section 125 plans, HRAs, or FSAs? They all have a separate set of laws to follow, and if you don't abide by every little detail, a government official might come knocking at your door.

And don't forget to manage your COBRA plan properly, or you could get sued by some disgruntled employee, that found the right lawyer, to work that side of the healthcare price system.

Now add on all of the federal and state taxes for everything. Do you think any of this affects the price of your health insurance?

"You betcha," as we say in Minnesota.

Price Analysis and Repricing

A new game is being played by employers across the nation, and it looks like this:

- Companies can now give their data to "in-the-know" consultants and allow them to use a company's claims data as leverage points against the main cost-drivers within their plans.
- They can zero in on the problem areas within a company's plan and present these findings to an employer.
- Then they can utilize these findings to present to national third-party administrators (TPAs), pharmacy benefit managers (PBMs), and many other healthcare providers in order to provide employers with much greater transparency in their pricing than ever before.
- In other words, they are using the free-market principles of choice and competition to determine where an employer and employee's money is best spent.
- There are even pre-priced healthcare contracts providing transparent (and *legally agreed upon*) pricing for any and all healthcare procedures. Remember, you are cash paying customers in the new 21st century world of employer sponsored healthcare.

Imagine if you owned a hospital and a company came to you with their 20,000 employees and said, "We'd be willing to recommend your hospital for all of our employees and their family members (which is likely a total of about 50,000 people when adding in spouses and dependents) if you'd be willing to write a separate contract with us, agreeing to a separate set of prices for all of the procedures you offer." What hospital wouldn't want a possible 50,000 new customers/patients coming in their doors when they need healthcare? Do you think those hospitals might even consider a more reasonable pre-priced healthcare arrangement? And, what if you told them that you will write into the contract that the hospital will get paid within 15-30 days for every procedure, instead of the normal "insurance-payment-system" of 90-180 days?

I hope you know these are rhetorical questions. And, these types of arrangements are happening all around the country between employers and hospital systems.

A new sweeping trend is providing cash-price modeling arrangements (without direct contracts even being written) that is saving companies millions of dollars. But these kinds of healthcare repricing programs do come with some disruptions. Most entrepreneurs and business owners understand that any real and meaningful change *never* happens without disruptions.

For instance, value-based (or reference-based) pricing models are being introduced all around America to great success. Consultants are using this model as a way of repricing healthcare and bringing down the cost of everything within one's healthcare plan. Value-based pricing uses the Medicare pricing models and adds an additional charge on top of those payments. Hospitals and other healthcare providers don't like the Medicare price models because the prices are so low. Value-based pricing is a way of providing hospitals and health providers a reasonable payment (for instance, they may agree to pay 170 percent of normal Medicare pricing) to give the providers enough to still make a profit. Employers may save as much as 40 to 60 percent on their healthcare pricing compared to a traditional self-insured PPO plan model. Many of these value-based pricing models can pay the healthcare providers in a much shorter time frame than having them sift through the normal health insurance red tape, only to be paid in three to six months, or even longer.

The down-side can be that some members may face something called "balanced billings," where a provider tells them that their procedure was not covered under their value-priced model plan. These members can unexpectedly receive "uninsured billings" in the mail for hundreds of thousands of dollars. Does the concept of having one of your employees come back to your HR director with a situation like this scare you? The "status quo" brokers and other players in the marketplace *want* you to be scared.

The truth is that these balanced billings only amount to 1 to 2 percent of an employer's population, but you still need to plan for these situations. The free market has already stepped up to provide a solution for balanced billing situations. Now you can pay a provider to negotiate these billings so that your employees don't have to be involved at all. Essentially this model takes on all financial liability so that neither your employees, or your company, has to deal with these messes. A qualified consultant will have already anticipated these kinds of issues and aligned your company with the proper ERISA attorneys and experienced TPAs to avoid these types of situations. By the way, ERISA references the Employee Retirement Income Security Act of 1974. Yes, another big rule and regulation.

When large companies of 10,000-plus employees are running $100 million healthcare budgets each year, these huge operating expenses can be transformed into earnings quickly by simply utilizing an in-depth audit that will reveal all that is hidden by a big insurance, big pharma, and big brokerage-firm plan.

Taking $30–$40 million from a normal $100-million operating-expense budget and transferring this directly to earnings can mean an enormous amount of money towards advancing a company's success and future. Remember, this is not just a first-year savings thing. This is an every-year savings thing!

Is $30–$40 million dollars of savings worth a little disruption to your 10,000-employee organization? You are the only one that can answer this question.

Saving money is a big part of the equation, but transforming the employees' healthcare benefits from $3,000 single/$6,000 family deductibles to *ZERO* deductibles and *ZERO* out-of-pocket costs would mean a lot to the company's employees and their families as well. Once a company gets its healthcare spending under control, it can immediately offer employees these low out-of-pocket alternatives to ease the pain employees have been experiencing for decades.

Small to midsize companies that choose to get out of the "risk-management" side of healthcare, and just provide tax-free money to their employees, are even using the Obamacare's healthcare exchange pricing to their advantage. You see, now that the exchanges have been up and running for six-plus years, individuals and families can get insurance policies at substantial discounts depending on their household incomes.

There are insurance agencies across America that have been working within the healthcare exchanges for 5+ years now. They know what they are doing and would be more than happy to help out any company that dares to go down this road. And they get paid for helping companies just like yours!

Combining the proper cafeteria plan strategy (mentioned in previous chapters) along with the discounted pricing of the Obamacare exchanges can produce some dramatic savings depending on your employees' incomes and demographics. To find out if this strategy is right for your company, your HR professional just needs to provide a census data report to one of the many qualified TPAs around the country to see what the numbers look like. The average health-insurance savings using this strategy is likely to be 40 to 60 percent when utilized properly.

These kinds of solutions are available right now in America, but almost no one knows about them. Worse yet, many of the "status quo players" out there in the marketplace don't want you to know about them.

I think you probably know why by now.

CHAPTER 10

THE ROLE OF BROKERS AND BROKERAGE FIRMS

Let me start out by stating unequivocally that it is extremely important to have a great brokerage firm on your side managing your benefits. The best brokerage firms use the highest levels of technology and strategies to help HR Directors offload as much responsibility as possible into the brokerage firms' hands, freeing up the HR professionals to actually deal with what they were hired to do—relating with humans, specifically the employees at your company. As consultants, we must be willing to develop relationships with all types of brokerage firms. There are literally thousands of brokerage firms all around the United States that assist companies of all sizes with a wide variety of employee benefits. Independent consultants have the ability to work with any brokerage firm in the nation, but a brokerage firm needs to be willing to cooperate and put the employer's and employee's interests first in designing a custom business healthcare design. If a CEO or CFO doesn't feel their brokerage firm is on their side, they simply can sign a few forms to put a different brokerage firm in charge that is looking out for their best interests.

Like with many professions, brokers and brokerage firms operate within their own sphere of existence. Most of them operate as if the HR person's only job exists within the employee-benefit space. Of course, HR professionals deal with so many other issues other than employee benefits that it boggles the mind. Typically, they supervise and provide consultation to management on staffing, compensation, training and development, budgets, and a wide variety of different labor relation issues that constantly battle the imperfect human condition (i.e., employees) on a daily basis.

Brokerage firms primarily help employers by coordinating and managing a wide array of employee benefits. There are many different kinds of benefits to incorporate: health, dental, vision, life, disability, HSAs, 401(k)s, workers' compensation, and a whole host of other related product vendors. A brokerage firm can help companies shop each marketplace and choose which vendors and which products are the right fit for a company and their employees.

The truly superior brokerage firms are introducing new solutions all the time. These solutions not only engage employees, but also improve efficiencies and provide employees with information at their fingertips to assist them in their daily lives. Technology, once again, is leading the way. Powerful tools and broad-based solutions are on the rise, with the leading technologies connecting employees with their benefits via their smartphones. These technologies connect employees directly with all of their benefits, freeing up the HR professional from their long list of responsibilities. Employees now can even utilize their smartphones to enroll, make changes to their benefits, and communicate directly with the insurance providers to eliminate the middle person (the HR professionals) and make everyone's job easier. If your employees can't access their benefits from their smartphones right now, I'm here to tell you that you are already behind the curve.

Some of the more advanced brokerage firms make it possible for your employees to access all of their benefits through a single website or a single phone app now. They also have staff available to answer employee questions about their benefit plans. This combination of twenty-first-century technology, along with actual living-breathing people, is still extremely valuable in the marketplace today.

Another key element to hiring a best-in-class brokerage firm is making a point to choose one that will ensure your business is fully compliant with the full range of rules and regulations (trust me, that list is long). Both health and welfare benefits and retirement plans have loads of compliance issues, which are confusing and difficult to navigate. Many times, a well-managed brokerage firm will have its own attorneys on staff who are well-versed in ERISA law and ACA regulations, as well as SEC and NASD requirements for retirement and 401(k) issues.

If you don't know what all of the aforementioned acronyms mean, then it's probably clear to you that you need an experienced brokerage firm that understands the ins-and-outs of every regulatory tier of your benefit package. Companies need to feel secure that they are being looked after and won't suffer any consequences by operating outside of any of the many compliance rules and regulations.

Compliance and benefit management are just one piece of the greater brokerage firm pie. Brokerage firms also provide the latest and greatest human resource information systems (HRIS) that allow efficient internal communications and easy onboarding and offboarding of employees for enrollment and COBRA situations.

Most people know that COBRA provides a right for employees to continue health coverage under their previous employer, should they leave employment. But did you know that employers are being sued periodically for not providing the proper COBRA notification forms (at the proper time) after an employee is let go? Former employees have sued their previous employers' countless times for not following the proper rules related to COBRA. This results in the employer paying hundreds of thousands of dollars for employees' insurance claims after an employee has already left a company, and experienced an accident or illness that resulted in massive hospital bills. The employer usually loses these disputes unless their brokerage firm's compliance team has their backs. Imagine having to face the reality of knowing that your insurance rates are increasing by 30 percent primarily because of a former employee's insurance claim?

Note to business owners: COBRA benefits would never be required if your employees owned their own healthcare coverage.

I have purposely taken the first part of this chapter to lay out all of the different elements that go into managing a good brokerage firm in order to make a relevant point. With so many responsibilities and categories to consider, how much time does a broker (within a brokerage firm) really have to focus on resolving and solving the business-healthcare issues that your company faces year-after-year?

Bottom line: brokers and brokerage firms are wearing way too many hats, and this poses a real problem.

Companies properly utilize brokerage firms to minimize the

time and effort needed to manage all of the many employee benefits.

But, ask yourself these questions:

1. What is your broker's role in specifically managing the healthcare program for your company and your employees? Are they monitoring and managing your claims each and every week?
2. Who are the internal "experts" within the different divisions of your brokerage firm responsible for all of the different benefits they manage?
3. Is your brokerage firm capable of putting their full focus and resources into a single category like business-healthcare management? And;
4. Is there an easy way to find out just how much my broker and brokerage firm is getting compensated for managing my healthcare and benefits?

Point #4 is certainly a difficult question to answer. As stated previously, some insurance products pay commissions (dental, life, disability, vision, voluntary insurance benefits) that are hidden from view. Some brokerage firms charge a consulting fee or a per-employee per-month (PEPM) fee that seems pretty transparent. How much in "persistency bonuses" does your brokerage firm receive by keeping you with one of the major insurance carriers? If you view your brokerage firm's primary responsibility as managing your health benefits, shouldn't you know *exactly* what they are receiving for this high-ticket responsibility?

Well, congress just passed (hidden within one of the stimulus bills) a new federal law called The Consolidated Appropriations Act of 2021. This will require health insurance agents, brokers, and brokerage firms to disclose all commissions and fees to current clients as well as prospects as of December 21st of 2021. Brokerage firms best be prepared to get ahead of this latest law or they could have some real egg on their faces. Exposing the actual fine print within some of these contracts will be quite eye-opening for many employers. These contracts often limit an employer's ability to access the data they need to analyze their spending, or restrict an employer's ability to audit their own claims. Most of these insurance companies don't want you to see all of the details of your own claims because employers can use this data to compare what else is out there in the marketplace. Keep this out-of-sight, and hopefully out-of-mind. Revealing the insurance company's and pharmacy company's revenue streams back to the brokers and brokerage firms may make your head explode. Each service provider may provide payments to brokers that might be unknown to the employer. For example, a pharmacy benefit manager might pay a broker a fee for every prescription filled under a health plan. Or a third-party administrator might give huge persistency bonuses back to the brokers just for convincing you to stay with the same warm cozy insurance company.

The good news is that **some** of these big brokerage firms have already revamped their contracts and revenue arrangements to come in line with these new regulations. But trying to find out which ones are actually doing this, is no easy task.

I came to realize that there is a specific need that isn't being satisfied in the marketplace. You wouldn't choose a general surgeon to perform knee, back, or heart surgery—you'd find a specialist, wouldn't you? Does it make sense to leave such important components of your business, and such a large part of your budget, up to a generalist rather than a specialist? A company with one hundred employees usually has a budget for healthcare of right around $1,000,000 to $1,500,000 each year. I believe this kind of money certainly deserves some special attention.

My goal (with this book) is to help you understand the working systems within most brokerage firms. The roles, responsibilities, and capabilities within any business decision are usually carefully analyzed before embarking on a long-term relationship. My point is that there should be a reasonably efficient system that allows a CEO or CFO to perform a detailed audit, with a reasonable SWOT (strengths, weaknesses, opportunities, and threats) analysis. Finding out who does what, and how much a broker or brokerage firm is being compensated for their particular efforts, seems reasonable to me.

The reality is that individual brokers are normally hired to bring new business to a brokerage firm. They are, at their very essence, salespeople. Once a typical broker acquires a new account, he or she is tasked with the responsibility of going out and getting more and more new accounts. Within most brokerage firms, no financial incentives exist to take the extra time to become familiar with the best methods for managing a healthcare plan for the companies they represent. In fact, the financial incentives are the opposite of what they should be today. And most brokers only think about what to do with their client's healthcare about three or four months prior to renewal time. That's the simple truth. This isn't the case for *every* broker at *every* brokerage firm, but sadly, it is for most.

Unfortunately, as an employer, you have no way to know which ones are getting great results on their healthcare management—and which ones are interested in only making a sale.

Bottom line: great ideas don't live under the brick and mortar of buildings called brokerage firms. Great ideas exist everywhere, and they are easier to access than ever before in our internet-connected world. However, you need to know where to look!

Our society is becoming more and more accustomed to managing our expectations and finding the best possible outcomes by referring to user reviews on sites like Amazon. We can get a quick glimpse by looking at star ratings or dig deeper and read specific customer feedback reviews. This is true for most products and services that consumers buy in the marketplace today, but that is not the case when it comes to finding the best brokers or brokerage firms for healthcare management.

I challenge you to go online today and find any brokerage firm that has reviews touting results from a particular broker within that firm who has had consistent success regarding their business clients' healthcare management. Even the biggest of brokerage firms refrain from posting measured results on their websites. After all, they are competing with other brokerage firms, and if none of the others post these kinds of results, why should they?

I embarked on this research journey six years ago, to try and understand how to resolve some of the massive healthcare-management issues facing our country. I realized early on that pigeon-holing myself into a broker's role at a brokerage firm was simply a limiting position. During this journey, I have only come across about 100 dedicated healthcare consultants spanning the United States. These are people who can actually illustrate past successes with their clients. Some of the ones I have found even display images on their websites of the business owners they represented, holding oversized refund checks in amounts of $250,000 or more right on their site. Have you seen any of these consultants' websites? Don't feel bad—you are not alone.

This is simply a system failure. The brokerage firm's systems are tasked to do a lot of extremely important things for their clientele. Businesses deserve someone who focuses their *full attention* on improving healthcare plans for their employees. Don't settle for anything less.

As a CEO, CFO, or HR professional, you should be asking yourself these questions:

- Does it make sense to consider hiring a specialist to specifically help analyze my healthcare budget and benefits?
- Is there any reason why I can't have a separate consultant for this purpose and keep my same brokerage firm to handle everything other than healthcare management?
- Investors pay investment-management teams loads of money each year to manage their investments to *make* them money. Wouldn't it make sense to hire a specialist to *save* money for something as large as your company's healthcare budget?

If your company's current brokerage firm has your healthcare spending under control, and you have no concerns over that part of your budget whatsoever, then you don't need an independent consultant to try to fix what isn't broken.

I am curious, though, why are you reading this book?

Maybe you are unsure as to whether or not your healthcare spending *is* under control. There is a very easy way to figure this out:

- Take your total amount of healthcare spending (make sure you include both employer and employee contributions) and divide that total annual amount by the number of employees you currently have on your healthcare plan.

- If that figure is more than $10,000 per employee per year, you are paying way too much.
- Some company's health insurance costs are approaching 40 to 50 percent of the employee's *total compensation*. Anyone think that is a moral position?

As I stated before, some companies are paying as much as $30,000 per employee per year. Companies like these can save more than $20,000 per employee per year. For companies with just 200 employees, this would calculate into $4,000,000 of first year savings, and *every single year from that point forward*. Do you see why this subject is so extremely critical at this point in time? Imagine what that kind of money would do for a company's bottom line? Do you think they may be able to give out some Christmas bonuses to all 200 employees come the end of the year?

I'm not saying you'll need to kick your current brokerage firm to the curb. They may still be the right choice to manage the host of all the other benefits you offer, saving your HR team a huge headache. The best (and, frankly, the most dedicated) healthcare consultants in the nation offer their services independent of a company's current brokerage firms. I like the type of consulting arrangements that pay the consultant only a percentage of what they save you as a company. Now that's real aligned incentives and true innovation!

Who knows, your broker might even be grateful to pass off the healthcare management to a specialized healthcare consultant. But don't be surprised if you meet some real resistance to this suggestion—and expect to seriously damage some egos along the way.

Brokers and brokerage firms are the distribution channels to all of the employers throughout the United States. The most exciting part of this new movement is that there are ways for brokers and brokerage firms to incorporate these new solutions into their business practices—and still survive (and possibly even thrive) well into the future. The big insurance companies will not welcome this kind of change. Many of the brokers and brokerage firms that have been hitching their wagons to these insurance companies' hidden compensation methods will not want to give up their gravy trains either.

Most brokers have not been educated properly on the newest solutions within the marketplace. But brokers beware: if you don't begin to sever yourselves from the commission and bonus relationships with the health-insurance companies, you may find yourselves in deep trouble in the future.

Brokers should not be receiving 20 percent raises when healthcare costs go up 20 percent for their employer clients. And it is simply wrong for insurance companies to be paying brokerage firms huge bonuses just to incentivize their brokers to renew and keep the business with a single insurance carrier. These misaligned incentives are being exposed, and the brokers who are still receiving commissions and bonuses this way will lose their clients' trust very quickly.

The bottom line is, brokerage firms are getting compensated indirectly from the insurance companies. But you (the customer) are paying for all of this mess. Shouldn't they be looking out for you, their customer? It's up to you to find the right people and the proper organizations to do the right job.

A final note on brokerage firms: the American consumer buys goods and services every day of their lives. Most people understand this simple calculation of: costs of goods + labor =

total price. Most businesses don't even know what the costs of goods + labor is for their broker or brokerage firm, let alone their total price. With literally millions of dollars changing hands every single year, and that "total price" being hidden from the employer's view by the insurance companies, how can you blame employers and their employees for being angry over this mess.

This is not just wrong, it's immoral.

Important Fact:
Before you go down the road of blaming your broker for this situation keep this fact in mind. When brokers enter into an insurance contract arrangement with an insurance company, that insurance company has the right to cancel a broker's contract *at any time*. Imagine yourself being a broker that has built up an income of $100,000+ with a particular insurance company. Would you want to tick-off that insurance company and have them cancel your contract, and leave you (and your family) without that income of $100,000+ each year?

As I stated earlier, this is a *system failure* and the incentives are misaligned. Most brokers don't understand how to get out of this system, even if they wanted to break away. After all, what kind of broker would welcome some third party stepping in and taking away their $100,000 - $200,000 income stream? See how disruptive this whole thing can be?

Now let me explain how you can turn this ship around.

CHAPTER 11

A DECLARATION OF "HEALTHCARE" INDEPENDENCE

The main problem we face in the twenty-first century is finding reliable and trustworthy answers to the many problems we face as human beings. But how can we trust most of the answers we get when they usually come in the form of a sales pitch? Seems like everyone is trying to sell us something—every single hour of every single day. We are faced with a barrage of commercials on TV or are constantly interrupted by ads on our computers, tablets, and smartphones. It's no wonder people are leery of anyone or any company that is trying to get our money.

But the health-insurance industry has devised a system of getting employers' and employees' money every single year, and getting us to accept the fact that we must pay more in premiums as well. This system makes us feel trapped because we can't compete as business owners unless we provide health coverage for our employees. To find out that the main players within this system have set things up to *intentionally* get more expensive while reducing the quality of healthcare for employees was maddening, to say the least. On top of all this mess, the government piled on and issued stiff penalties to both businesses and individuals for not buying health insurance the way "they think we should buy it."

All that has changed as of January 1st, 2020. Freedom of choice is flourishing in the business-healthcare communities of America. This book lays out some of the hidden solutions that can be adopted immediately. No more getting pushed around by forces that are not looking out for you. It's time to find your own freedoms. Set sail on your own course, and realize the significant savings and control over your business healthcare waiting for you on the other side.

The following is a brief recap of your new freedom solutions.

- PEOs – Professional-Employer Organizations
  - Designed for businesses wishing to outsource their employee benefits to provide a broader variety of benefits while carving out their healthcare to customize it to match their own philosophy. Primarily a good fit for employers with 10 -150 employees.
- Custom Health Plans
  - Unique self-insured plan designs that unbundle the elements of a healthcare plan. Using cost-and-contain strategies, custom plans control the main cost-drivers within a health plan (prescription drugs, outpatient surgeries, hospital costs, and primary care expenses), getting a handle on the number, size, and frequency of your employee's claims. Custom plans

give you more control over the underlying *healthcare costs* that have been driving employers' *health insurance costs* up for decades. These designs are attractive to both the "C Suites" as well as HR professionals because all of your administrative systems can remain the same. Custom plans will be initially attractive for employers with 50-500 employees. Companies of this size can choose to apply for the new Coalition plan designs. These Coalition plans allow these mid-sized companies to join in with other like-minded employers and be a part of much larger populations to substantially reduce their risks. But when companies of 500 to 5000+ employees begin to clue into the advantages of custom plan designs, it will change the face of healthcare forever.

- Cafeteria-Plan Designs
  - Breaking free from the traditional employer-owned contract, the cafeteria plan provides tax-free money to employees and allows them to customize their coverage to fit their own particular needs. This cuts off the head of the snake, connecting employers to insurance contracts, and disconnects employers from employee's claims management completely. This also opens the floodgates to the vast number of choices available to individual employees today, that were never available to them before. This will initially be attractive to the small to mid-sized marketplace. But once again, if the larger companies of 1000+ employees start to compare with their old 1942 employer-owned plans, all bets are off.

Custom Health Plans – The Natural First Choice

Most companies of larger sizes will usually explore the custom health-plan design first because it won't change how a company currently administers its health plans. The HR director can operate using the exact same systems they are currently using. None of the employees will be disrupted (either during or after the change), and the result will be better healthcare benefits, allowing you the choice of reducing down the premiums for your employees.

Most large companies are already operating within a self-insured design. But most have never even heard of the new custom plan designs due to the recent adoption of these unique methods. This still means that companies operate as if they have a "mini insurance company" within their organization, but even the largest of organizations are not running their "mini health insurance plans" with any meaningful spending controls.

Remember, 80-90 percent of a self-insured plan's cost comes from paying their own claims out of this big bucket of cash called "corporate earnings" each and every month. Most companies get hung up on trying to lower the 10-20 percent they are spending on their administrative *fixed-cost bucket* and don't realize the main focus should be on the much higher percent *variable-spending bucket*.

Now, it may seem like a no-brainer to you (the reader) that if you are the CEO of a 20,000-employee company spending a total of $200 million each year on healthcare, in which $170 million was spent on paying all of your claims out of the earnings of your company, that the focus should be on the $170 million right?

Well, you'd be surprised to know that most times, it has never even been suggested to either the CEO or the CFO that they can truly control the spending out of this big bucket of money.

An independent consultant, who is connected to the proper supporting vendors, can perform free audits and allow you to see how sick your group health plan actually is by overlaying your claims history with what the "freedom vendors" can deliver. Since many of these consultants are writing contracts that only charge clients *a percentage of what they save a company*, businesses can now step into this space without taking on any unnecessary financial risks.

My advice to most any company of substantial size would generally be this:

You've likely been self-insured for some years now—it's time to start acting like it!

It's really not that difficult to get the attention of the CEO or CFO of a company once they know their results could be a 20 to 40 percent reduction to their $200 million annual healthcare spend each and every year. Especially when you inform them that it is already being done by hundreds of companies just like them, all around the country, to great success.

The hardest part is getting employers to see that hourglass turned upside down, uncovering all of the solutions waiting for them on the other side. As I mentioned in the first chapter, most insurance companies, pharmacy companies, and brokerage firms want you to see the business-healthcare world through "their distribution-channel eyes" and not anyone else's.

PEOs – The One-Two Punch Choice

A professional-employer organization (PEO) seems like a no-brainer at first blush. Having a separate firm doing most all of the administrative work to provide a wider array of benefits to employees is truly a big step forward. But, of course, like any product or service in the marketplace, it comes with a price. The average cost for a PEO can range from $900 to $1,500 per employee per year. Some employers choose to be charged a percentage of payroll. This can range between 3 to 10 percent of your total payroll, depending on the PEO.

Not all PEOs allow a company to carve out health insurance within their solution, yet this is a rapidly changing environment as well. Capturing the health insurance within a PEO can produce substantial commissions back to the PEO firms. Many PEOs are reluctant to give up these revenue streams. Just know that if you allow the PEO to manage your employees' healthcare, they will be in control of your healthcare plan, not you. Their systems of healthcare management are really no different than the typical retail-health-insurance plans that go up in price—and down in benefits.

New in the marketplace for employers are PEO brokerage firms. These are companies that allow you to shop the marketplace to find the best fit for your particular PEO needs.

You may be a trucking company that needs help with your workers' compensation costs and your healthcare program. You may be a law firm that has low workers' compensation costs but needs help managing payroll and compliance issues and likes the idea of someone else managing your 401(k). PEO brokerage firms can design a program around your needs and then fit you with the proper PEO that comports with your particular problem areas.

Most companies that fall into the category of 10 to 150 employees find that the additional costs of the PEO are well worth it. Once you get above the 150-employee level, your HR department may be able to handle the additional administrative services offered by the PEO. This cost/benefit analysis is a relatively easy calculation to make to determine whether or not your company has outgrown your PEO.

I call this solution the one-two punch solution because utilizing the proper PEO solution, along with either a custom health-plan or cafeteria health-plan design, can provide employers with a dramatic change to their administrative functions *and* control their healthcare budget at the same time.

Important note: The PEO solution can incorporate either the custom health-plan design or the cafeteria-plan design, as long as the PEO allows a health carve-out option for the employer.

Cafeteria-Plan Designs – The Game-Changing Choice

"We must not focus our attention exclusively on the material, because though important, it is not the main issue. The economic success of the Western world is a product of its moral philosophy and practice. The economic results are better because the moral philosophy is superior. *It is superior—because it starts with the individual.*" — **Margaret Thatcher**

Though every business will be free to choose their own particular road, I believe the cafeteria plan provides a superior path that could potentially change the business-healthcare landscape in America. Allow me to explain why.

Once a business breaks away from a traditional offering of employer-owned health insurance, it opens the door to allow employees to price their own health-care coverage. And if you are an employee who qualifies for a discount on your insurance plan through one of the nationwide insurance exchanges (these have been up and running for over six years now), you may be eligible for a substantial reduction in your health insurance premiums.

*Extremely Important Note: Your employees **may** not be eligible for these discount-priced insurance plans through the exchanges if you (the employer) still offer an employer-owned group-insurance plan of any kind. Make sure to consult a qualified ERISA attorney about hybrid-plan models before implementing this type of arrangement.*

Here are the income levels to qualify for premium subsidies:

Household Size	Income Level
1	$50,040
2	$68,960
3	$86,880
4	$104,800
5	$122,720
6	$140,640

If your employees' household incomes are below these levels, they qualify for a discount on their health insurance premiums. How much of a discount?

Let me provide some examples:

Say you are a single guy (age 30) making $30,000 a year. Normally your premium would be $300 to $500 a month for an average $3,000 deductible silver program through an employer-owned plan. Since this person is just making $30,000 a year, the premium gets dropped to $195 a month for the same silver plan through the individual exchange. He still owns the same coverage, but because his income falls below the qualifying amount of $51,040, he receives a subsidy or discount for his individually owned plan.

How about a divorced single mom of forty-three years old with two kids earning just $32,000 a year? If she applied for coverage through her work, her insurance cost for the same $3,000 deductible silver plan may be somewhere around $700 to $900 per month. But because she's only making $32,000 a year, her premium goes down to $106 a month for that same individually owned silver plan through the healthcare exchange.

Now let's say you have a family of four with two adults (both age 42) and two kids, with a combined income of $61,000. Average family coverage through an employer-owned plan may cost between $1,400 to $1,700+ per month for that $3,000 deductible silver plan. But since their combined income is only $61,000 a year, their premium gets dropped to $392 a month for the same silver plan. A savings of over $1,000 per month.

You see, if you just play by the rules that the government and the insurance companies have laid out before us, you can beat them at their own game! They made the rules. But now you're playing the new freedom game. Oh wait, it gets better. Much Better!

Anyone who qualifies for this discount-priced healthcare through the exchanges can take advantage of another ACA/Obamacare ruling. This law states that you will never pay more than a certain percentage of your income for your part of the insurance premiums. And now, the Biden administration just passed a law stating that no person or family will have to pay any more than 8.5% of their income on health insurance for the next two years. In case you fell asleep, and weren't paying attention to that previous sentence, let me make sure you hear me.

IF YOU BUY AN INDIVIDUALLY-OWNED HEALTH INSURANCE PLAN FOR THE YEAR OF 2021 AND 2022, NO ONE PERSON OR FAMILY WILL PAY ANY MORE THAN 8.5% OF THEIR HOUSEHOLD INCOME.

If this legislation stands up in years 2023 and beyond, this will also mean that your individual premiums will increase ONLY if your household income goes up.

I know that sounds completely goofy, but this is all part of the new game that the government is laying out for us. And remember, the insurance companies can't ask medical questions for individuals applying for health insurance anymore. So, employers may have to do some extra leg work (initially) in order to transform their coverage into a cafeteria-plan design, but remember, employees no longer need to worry about anybody being disqualified when applying for this type of insurance coverage. It's not that difficult to run a census evaluation to determine what your employees can get for coverage compared to your group insurance plan. Find out who qualifies for discounts and who doesn't, and compare these prices with a current group insurance plan.

Does this sound a little too good to be true again? Oh wait, I'm not even close to being done.

Now that you've done a proper financial evaluation of how many employees qualify for standard coverage and how many qualify for the discount-priced coverage through the exchanges, you will have a chance to see how much your savings could be compared to your current employer-owned plan.

Let's do some simple math again. Your 100-employee-company was paying $1,100,000 under your corporate retail health plan.

Under this plan, it was a crapshoot as to how much the premiums would go up every year. Now, under your new cafeteria design, your new total premiums are $600,000 a year. Let's just assume for a moment that, on average, all of your employees signed up for that same $3000-deductible silver plan. As an employer, you also have the freedom to put money into an account that helps them with their deductibles. Let's say you fund $250 a month (or $3,000 a year, equal to that same $3,000 deductible) into a health flexible-spending account (FSA)—or even better, a health savings account (HSA)—for every employee.

So now, your new plan costs are:

$600,000 in premiums + $300,000 HSA = $900,000

Now, you've reduced most everyone's premiums, you've funded all employees' deductibles for the first year into nice new HSA swipe-cards for everyone to pay their healthcare bills, and you've saved your company $200,000. Oh, by the way, your new budget of $600,000 for premiums and $300,000 for your new HSA plan is *completely under your control* now. If business goes well, you can choose to increase your budget next year. If your business doesn't go so well, you can back off of your budget if necessary. But never again will an insurance company come back to you at the dreaded "renewal time" to tell you that your budget needs to increase because your rates are going up again. You may just decide next year to reduce down your HSA contributions from $300,000 to $150,000, since HSA dollars rollover year after year. You've already funded everyone's deductibles in the first year anyway.

Then in the sub-sequent year you may decide to take another path.

You may offer a dollar-for-dollar match of your HSA contributions if your employees participate and contribute some of their own money towards their program. See how having the employees own their own coverage starts to get them more involved by simply having them take on a little more responsibility? The more control they have, the less you (the employer) need to concern yourself with their personal choices. You will eventually have the choice to drop your company's HSA contributions down to zero to let them contribute as they feel necessary. In essence, you've now allowed them to grow up and given them the freedom to control their own destinies.

Individual health-insurance rates differ within each state. So, make sure you have your healthcare consultant perform a proper census-price analysis in case you have a company with employees in multiple states. But here's an even simpler calculation. Take the gross salaries of all of your employees combined (that are on your health plan now) and multiply this total number times 8.5 percent. Subtract this figure from what you are currently paying annually for your employer-owned health insurance. You will see how much potential savings there could be, should you simply choose to have your employees own their own coverage going forward.

The cold hard fact is, once you fully convert to the cafeteria-plan design, you *literally* don't have a business-healthcare renewal anymore—because you don't own the insurance contract.

I could keep going to describe how you could also incorporate a business health-sharing choice for your healthy employees who don't mind answering a few medical questions. I could tell you about how, if they qualify, your employees could get a $500 deductible plan that has monthly premiums amounts that look like this:

Single	$189
Single + spouse	$434
Single + children	$380
Family	$631

But you probably don't want to hear about this just now. Maybe a little too much freedom for one day?

Well, it's my book, and I'm telling you anyway.

CHAPTER 12

MOVE OVER BIG INSURANCE, BIG FREEDOM'S TAKING OVER

Health-sharing operates exactly like a regular health-insurance program with some caveats for pre-existing health conditions. Most companies require a broad list of medical questions in order to qualify. This is evolving, however. Some health-share companies are now choosing to accept everyone with some limitations on coverage. For instance, if you've had a heart attack, stroke, or cancer within the past 3-5 years, you may not receive coverage for those particular conditions should you choose to accept coverage on a health share plan. You would be covered for most any other medical condition, but if you had a pre-existing condition you would have to go "treatment free" for 3-5 years before receiving full coverage related to those particular conditions. Some health-sharing companies provide an ever-increasing amount of coverage for those pre-existing conditions for a set period of time. For instance, if you previously had prostate cancer and signed up for health sharing coverage, you would receive zero coverage for that prostate cancer (should it re-occur) in the first year. Second year you may receive $25,000 of coverage. And third year $50,000 worth of coverage should you need to be treated for prostate cancer again. If you make it all of the way past year three, you will receive 100% coverage for not only your prostate cancer (should it re-occur) but for anything else that may go wrong with your health. Should this trend continue to evolve, who knows how many Americans will choose this as an option over the high-priced health insurance alternatives. As it sits right now, 70 to 80 percent of the population will qualify and choose health sharing over health insurance. I know of one outstanding consulting firm (out on the east coast) that placed 40 new companies in 2020 using this model, allowing employees to choose either health insurance or health sharing coverage within their cafeteria design. On average 70 percent chose the health sharing plans out of the population of all 40 companies combined.

Health sharing operates by large groups of people buying into a strategy where each member is responsible for a certain portion of their healthcare claim payments, similar to a $500 or $1,000 deductible for standard health-insurance contracts, and the rest of the claim is paid for by the health-sharing group as a whole.

The health-sharing programs don't call themselves *health insurance* at all. They do this on purpose. They operate under a specific loophole that allows them to *legally* share costs with their members without being subject to the horrific rules and regulations that are levied on insurance companies by the federal and state governments. Interesting, huh?

How can they do this? Remember the story I told you in the first few chapters about how 1,000 people in a town all chipped in to share in each other's medical expenses? Health-sharing companies use this same concept, but many of these companies operate with well over 100,000 people in them, not 1,000. The health-sharing plan my wife and I were covered under in 2018 had over 400,000 members in it—and has been growing ever since. In fact, the marketplace is so ripe for these innovative health-plan designs that one health-sharing company has grown from 15 employees to over 350 employees within just the last two years. And there are no networks. You can go anywhere you want in order to receive the best medical care possible. And isn't that the way it should be?

The costs of these individual health-sharing programs are also extremely affordable. They range anywhere from $50 to $200 for a single person and from $450 to $800 for an entire family per month (no matter how many kids you have by the way). The levels of coverage range from $500 to $2,500 for the out-of-pocket expenses when members experience a claim. Once an individual hits his or her out-of-pocket expense, the rest is shared by the collective "health-sharing pool."

But these health-share plans aren't allowed to call their payments *premiums*, so they go by the name *shared amounts* for legal purposes.

See the game? Can't call it *insurance*. Can't call it *premiums*. If you do, you open the floodgates for all of the nasty rules and regulations that make health insurance so expensive. But the concept of insuring members is exactly the same. It's just not listed under the banner of health insurance.

The two drawbacks to the health-sharing programs are:

1. They are required to operate on an after-tax basis, and
2. You do have to answer a list of medical questions.

You see, they do apply the old school risk-management principles, just as any normal insurance program is supposed to operate. You may think this is a deal-breaker, but when 70-80 percent of America would get past these medical questions and qualify for the coverage, the after-tax issue quickly becomes a non-factor. And when you consider the huge cost difference, this is many times a no-brainer.

Remember, my wife and I were about to pay $1,800 a month for our pre-tax group-insurance program with a $4,000 deductible way back in August of 2018. We ended up taking a health-share program that cost $344 a month for the two of us, with a $500 out-of-pocket max for any medical occurrence. After comparing the $1,800 a month pre-tax payment with our $344 a month after-tax payment, it didn't take us long to decide this was a better deal. This has saved us over $30,000 in premiums over the last two years alone.

If a company adopted a cafeteria plan that offered individual health-insurance coverage, *subsidized* health-insurance-exchange coverage, and a health-sharing option, this would allow employees to choose which is best for them and their families. Giving your employees the ***moral respect*** of allowing them their own "freedom of choice" opens the door for you (the employer) to enjoy your own freedoms, and to operate independently from the system that has been crushing employers and their employees for decades.

Compare this type of program to a traditional employer-owned retail plan in the marketplace. You will see that some companies are paying $700 to $900 a month for a single employee and as much as $1,700 to $2,200 a month for family coverage. This is for coverage with $3,000 deductibles for singles and $6,000 deductibles for families—with the out-of-pocket costs being $8,000 for singles and $16,000 for families.

Today, seven to ten different health-sharing choices are available in the marketplace. They are competing for your business both in the personal as well as the business marketplace now. They also provide experienced TPA's (third-party administrators) to negotiate all claims for their members, and they all operate from a cash-paying position rather than the exhaustingly ridiculous PPO health insurance nonsense that has been breaking the backs of Americans for decades.

Keep in mind: this is relatively new to the employer marketplace. You don't have to offer this health-sharing choice to your employees as one of your "employer offerings." This offering requires a lot more education than meets the eye. I believe it will still take some years for this to take hold in the employer-healthcare space. But any employee can choose an individual health-sharing program right now if they want to. The problem is that if you (the employer) are currently paying 100 percent of your employees' premiums under your old retail health-plan model, then why would any of your employees ever think to choose any other plan but your employer coverage? Even if your program stinks, your employees will almost never pass up an insurance plan that is essentially free to them.

Will the *health-sharing* industry evolve to eventually take over the *health-insurance* industry? Who knows for sure? But if they keep improving their models and folks keep on looking for lower-cost alternatives in the marketplace, the entire health-insurance industry may be at risk. Think about it, if you were a family of four or five, and covered under your family plan at work, it might cost you $1,200 a month even after your boss paid $500 of the premium. Now if he offered you a health-sharing plan for $700 a month wouldn't you at least want to know more about this coverage? And, if your boss then said that he'd pay the same $500 (that he paid before) of your new $700 a month health-sharing plan, wouldn't you **_really_** want to know more?!

When you take the time to think it through, your employees buy everything else in the marketplace that fits their own needs. In other categories of insurance, they can buy their own life insurance, dental insurance, car insurance, and homeowners' insurance. Would it be so bad if you allowed them to buy their own health insurance or healthcare coverage on their own? Why should health insurance be any different?

You do pay them good money to work for your company. They are capable of making every other buying decision on their own in the marketplace. Why not give them the opportunity to make their own healthcare and health insurance decisions as well? You're free to pay them a respectable wage—allow them the freedom to buy what they want.

By simply shifting this *one decision* and allowing your employees a choice to *own their own coverage*, it provides a *dramatic economic shift* that opens up an entire world of new choices, better coverage, and lower prices.

The cafeteria design may not be the right fit for every situation (or every employer), but wouldn't it make sense to look at all angles to see if this might make sense for your company?

All of these new healthcare business models exist in the marketplace today. There are consultants, ERISA attorneys, TPAs, insurance agents, and even the health-sharing companies that are ready to assist you in transforming your company's broken healthcare plan into a twenty-first-century design.

I did mention that they are all looking for your business? I did, didn't I?

Most employers just want to know three basic things to *even consider* changing gears on their employee healthcare.

These are:

1. Is it legal?
2. How disruptive will these solutions be to my employees and my HR team? And;
3. Have these solutions performed successfully in the marketplace to the satisfaction of other employers?

Truth or Consequences

Once employers have answered the above three questions to their satisfaction, they simply need to know the truth.

Truth #1 – Great solutions exist outside the narrow distribution channels of brokers and brokerage firms.

Truth #2 – Employers can take control of the cost-drivers within any health plan and dramatically reduce their spend on healthcare within custom plan designs.

Truth #3 – Employers can legally provide tax-free money to their employees (regardless of the employee size) and allow them to buy exactly the type of coverage they want for their families.

Truth #4 – There are no pre-existing conditions for either employer or employee when buying health insurance under the law in 2021.

Truth #5 – Companies are providing zero-deductible health plans for employees right now in the marketplace.

Truth #6 – Under the new cafeteria-plan designs, no one employee can ever have a high claim that affects any another employee's rates or benefits . . . Ever!

Owners of companies can face these truths and utilize them to their advantage or face the consequences of having one or more of their competitors adopt these strategies and risk losing valuable employees to them in the future. The other consequences of not embracing these truths will be ever-increasing prices and ever-decreasing benefits for you and your employees.

"I paid my consultant $1,500,000, and it didn't cost me a dime."

- Quote from a brave and disrupting "Future CEO"

This is a "future interview story" with a CEO that got fed up with the entire mess of healthcare, and finally took serious action.

Interviewer: "Tell me a little bit about your company's story, and how you saved $50,000,000 on your employee's healthcare in just 18 months"

CEO: "I met an entrepreneur consultant two years ago that convinced me to start looking at my business healthcare through different eyes. He started by laying out some basic facts about my company, and established a framework of thinking that started me down an extremely interesting road."

"We established that my 10,000-employee company was spending just north of $100,000,000 a year on our healthcare, and had seen average increases of 4%-6% each year over the last decade. He asked me if I had ever heard of a framework of thought called "first principal" thinking? I told him I thought I had heard Elon Musk mention this in relation to the development of the batteries he had constructed for his Tesla electric cars. YES, he exclaimed!

He wanted me to boil things down to first establish the most fundamental truths, the things that we *absolutely knew to be true* regarding my business healthcare, and then reason up from there. He explained that this was actually more of a physics way of thinking about the world, and he wanted me to apply this critical thought process to my healthcare."

Interviewer: "Did he give you some examples of other ways of thinking regarding this topic, and what his experience was in that regard?"

CEO: "He stated that most people reason by analogy. In other words, they try to resolve issues or problems based upon "what other people have done", or "what others are currently doing". He said that it is much easier to reason by analogy, than to reason by first principals. He explained that analogy thinking is a standard thought process, and is the easiest, least time-consuming way of thinking.

I found out that it actually takes a lot more time and mental energy to reason from a first principal standpoint than I originally thought, but he assured me it would be worth my time."

The following was a list of the 5 first principals of my business healthcare:

1. I currently owned my healthcare contract, not my employees.
2. The cumulative "health" of all my employees and their family members determined the future costs of my business healthcare, and that a small percentage of my employees (6%-10%) accounted for 80% of all of our claims.
3. If my employees all owned their own coverage, the future claims of my employees could never financially impact me (the employer) because we would

not be playing the "risk management role" anymore. Furthermore, any one person's high claim would not "infect" any other employees or their family members.

4. There were legal ways to allow a small portion of the population (within our firm) to beta-test the cafeteria design, and perform a cost/benefit analysis afterwards, to compare our current employer-owned plan to the individually owned healthcare models.

5. The consultant's ERISA attorneys could provide solid planning (and formal documentation) to satisfy all of the government's requirements to avoid any penalties or fees to my firm.

Interviewer: "So, what were your next steps once you established these first principals?"

CEO: "We beta-tested a portion of our population. We decided to test the salaried employees first since they were agreeable to the process. There were approximately 200 salaried employees that were given the choice to break away from our group and apply for what fit their situation the best. The choice was either individual health insurance or a health-sharing plan. They ended up splitting almost right down the middle with 100 choosing insurance, and 100 choosing health-sharing.

Interviewer: "What was the ultimate price tag for the 200 employees, compared to what they were paying on your group plan?"

CEO: "The total cost ended up being 48% less with most everyone receiving, in their own words, better coverage."

Interviewer: "Wow, so what did you end up doing next?"

CEO: "I sat down with my leadership team and asked them what the struggles had been with our beta-test group, and whether they thought this might be too challenging to attempt with the entire company? The overwhelming consensus was that with so much in premium savings, they would work through any and all issues, and our HR team would make sure the employees were happy in every way on the back-side of this whole thing."

Interviewer: "So even though you anticipated the dramatic savings coming soon for all of your employees, was it an administrative nightmare?"

CEO: "We definitely had our challenges during the transition, but we had the proper solution partners in place to assist my leadership team with any and all issues that came to bear. We all agreed that we've had issues before with other transitions, but this was going to be worth the extra effort."

Interviewer: "So, what does the future look like now for your healthcare and your business in general?"

CEO: "My employees seem to really love the new model. We've implemented a strong HSA program that drops tax-free money into their swipe cards every month to help them pay their co-pays and deductibles. Best of all, my CFO has our costs under control for the first time in decades, and she can focus more on our business at hand now."

Interviewer: "Last question, how was it that you paid your healthcare consultant $1,500,000 and it didn't cost you a dime?"

CEO: "He ended up agreeing to only taking a small percentage of our savings, to quarterback the entire deal."

Interviewer: "What percentage did he agree to, and how much did you ultimately save?"

CEO: "We ended up saving a total of $50,000,000 compared to our previous budget that was $100,000,000 just 18 months ago. And believe it or not, the consultant agreed to just 3 percent of our *savings amount*, not 3 percent of our total healthcare budget. We had no real financial risk, since he based his compensation on the amount of our savings, and nothing more.

I liked that arrangement because the more we saved, the more he made. And I can honestly tell you he worked his ass off!"

Interviewer: "So, do you expect your healthcare budget to be $50,000,000 from this point forward?"

CEO: "You know, I actually believe it will be even lower next year."

Interviewer: "And why is that?"

CEO: "Because some of our employees weren't totally comfortable with trusting the new health-sharing option for the first year. We will have another meeting in about 6 months to get feedback from the folks who chose the health-sharing coverage to see how they liked it. If we get an overall favorable response, we believe more and more people will end up choosing the health-sharing option that was much less expensive and provided better overall coverage. "We already calculated that if 20% more of our people choose the health-sharing coverage next year our health care budget will likely drop to around $38,000,000. I like the idea that our business healthcare budget is flat, unless we decide to raise it ourselves now."

How far off into the future is the possibility of an interview like this to really happen?

The way things are set up now....... *It could be next* *week!*

Closing Comments

This book is not just about freedom and the proper use of the free-market system to help save healthcare in America. It's about a belief in the *redeeming moral value of freedom*, which I believe should apply not only to our economic lives but to every other aspect of our lives. Each of us makes multiple economic decisions over the course of our everyday lives. The degree that you take away a person's ability to choose, you are taking away their moral agency, or in other words, their freedom. Business owners are free to spend their hard-earned money as they see fit. Let's face it, health-insurance premiums have been hiding (in a most sinister way) inside your employee's payroll checks, eating into the take-home pay of American workers long enough.

Look at it this way: we all want to raise our children to become self-reliant, strong, and productive citizens, right? We'd also like them to have a strong sense of morality as well. Yet, in order to achieve these things, we must eventually allow them to leave the nest to be free to choose the proper paths for themselves.

Not every child makes wise decisions as he grows older and recognizes his own path. But, allowing them this *freedom to choose* is the key to growth and maturity in life.

Adam Smith wrote two books, The Theory of Moral Sentiments and The Wealth of Nations. The Wealth of Nations introduced a free-market economic framework for societies to follow. But Smith also understood that you need a moral compass with which to guide these societies, so he wrote The Theory of Moral Sentiments to provide that guiding perspective. Just as our founders drafted the Constitution with the moral guidance of God's hand in mind, Adam Smith's two books offered sound moral principles guided by the economic "invisible hand" of freedom.

But something as big as business healthcare can't be left to sifting through a "sales system" to try and figure out what works and what doesn't. We need trustworthy, reliable, and affordable knowledge. And we need it *now!*

This is the real reason why I chose to write this book.

More than half of the people in the United States are insured through their employers nationwide. It is my mission to get this knowledge into the eyes and ears of as many businesses as possible. Allowing employers to recognize their freedoms in this space can literally change America.

Shameless Plug

I made some claims in Chapter 1.

I promised after reading this book you would:

1. Understand the innovative business-healthcare solutions that already exist around the country with proven track records of success.
2. Be able to connect with the proper solution partners for efficient implementation into your business.
3. Know the exact steps you need to take to save 20 to 40 percent or more in healthcare and health insurance costs within 120 days.

If there's one thing I really hate about today's world of "so called" problem solvers, is when someone gives you a 3-to-5 step plan on solving something, only to find out later that you need to do a ton of work yourself to solve this particular problem.

In order for me to deliver on my promises I want everyone to understand some basic facts. It would take a very long time for anyone to research and develop all of the information that I have gathered over the last six to ten years.

If I left all of this in my reader's hands you would have to decide for yourself:

1. Which philosophy is the best fit for me and my company?
2. Which solution partner matches up with my size of company, and in my particular industry and location?
3. Which consultant, broker, or brokerage firm is designed "with the proper systems" to help me transform my health plan?

As I stated before, my role is as a super-connector to fast-track your health plan conversion. I provide this with my own "set of systems" to get you to the other side as quickly and painlessly as possible.

I run high-level RFPs with the same efficiencies as I advocate for any of my solution partnerships around the country.

Our RFP technology system is equipped to ask the proper questions, include the proper solution partners, and is even designed to include your current brokerage firm on the RFP to be fair.

Here's a list of the top 10 brokerage firms in the United States according to an article in Business Insurance magazine as of January 21st, 2021. All of these deliver outstanding service to all of their clients within their blocks of business.

Marsh & McLennan Cos. Inc.
Aon P.L.C.
Willis Towers Watson P.L.C.
Arthur J. Gallagher
HUB International
Brown & Brown, Inc.
Truist Insurance Holdings Inc.
Lockton Inc.
Acrisure
USI Insurance LLC

There are over 36,000 different brokerage firms across the United States. Do you know which brokers, within any of these many brokerage firms, that are consistently saving an average of 20%-40% for their employer clients on healthcare?

Once you've determined which philosophy fits your firm, we fast-track you to these exact brokers and brokerage firms, and include them on your RFP.

Remember, it simply comes down to puzzles and math. We help you put the right puzzle pieces in place, and then it's just simple math.

Our fast-track RFP saves an average of $2,300 per employee per year. That's $230,000 if you're a company of just 100 employees. Whether you're a company of 100, 1000, or 10,000 employees, you can do the math.

But if you're concerned about hurting the feelings of a broker or brokerage firm, don't even bother contacting us. We are extremely dedicated to providing results, and cannot concern ourselves over disgruntled status-quo brokers, insurance companies, or pharmacy providers.

Here's our website: www.jb-benefits.com

Eventually all of this knowledge will be offered online through affordable 3-part webcasts, online-seminars, and even mastermind classes for brokers who are interested in changing their business models, along with the rest of the business healthcare world. If we can change the distribution channel, we will change America.

Systems Produce Winners
Dreams without goals are just dreams. Goals without systems become unrealized goals. Systems are what makes dreams come true. Every one of the solutions that you have read about within this book is backed by companies that have incorporated carefully planned out *systems*. Plugging your company into any one of these systems will produce results. But don't expect someone else to do all of the work for you. You and your team must roll up your sleeves and be ready to work in order for these systems to produce the results you want to achieve.

It's time for a major change to disrupt this sinister system. In my mind, these changes can't come quickly enough—but that's just me.

I think health insurance sucks.

ACKNOWLEDGEMENTS

I first want to acknowledge the people that I most admire for their outstanding abilities in the arena of critical thinking. Critical thinking is becoming a rarity in the world today, and is actually being vilified among many circles within our societies. I very much doubt that Albert Einstein would be lifted up as a genius today, should he had been born within this generation.

Besides the obvious greats of the far-off past like Aristotle, Plato and Nietzsche, I'd like to also acknowledge the founders of this great country. Without these original thinkers, none of us may have been able to write (or even talk) about anything related to freedom today.

This short list of brilliant minds has made more of an impact on me than words can express. They not only bring brilliance to their particular fields of expertise, but also possess the ability to bring their critical thought process to almost any subject matter. A true rarity in our society today.

Thanks to all of these people for making my world (and the broader world in general) a richer and more vibrant place to live.

Listed in order from oldest to youngest:

- Adam Smith
- Milton Friedman
- Thomas Sowell
- Dennis Prager
- Patrick Bet David
- Alex Epstein